Bernard Malamud Revisited

Twayne's United States Authors Series

Warren French, Editor

University College of Swansea, Wales

TUSAS 601

BERNARD MALAMUD
© *Jerry Bauer*

Bernard Malamud Revisited

Edward A. Abramson

University of Hull

Twayne Publishers • New York
Maxwell Macmillan Canada • Toronto
Maxwell Macmillan International • New York   Oxford   Singapore   Sydney

PS3563
A4
Z498
1993

Bernard Malamud Revisited
Edward A. Abramson

Copyright © 1993 by Twayne Publishers.

Twayne Publishers   Maxwell Macmillan Canada Inc.
Macmillan Publishing Company   1200 Eglinton Avenue East
866 Third Avenue   Suite 200
New York, New York 10022   Don Mills, Ontario M3C 3N1

Macmillan Publishing Company is a member of the Maxwell Communication Group
of Companies.

Library of Congress Cataloging-in-Publication Data

Abramson, Edward A.
    Bernard Malamud revisited / Edward A. Abramson.
        p.   cm. — (Twayne's United States authors series : TUSAS 601)
    Includes bibliographical references and index.
    ISBN 0-8057-7641-9 (alk. paper)
    1. Malamud, Bernard—Criticism and interpretation.   I. Title.
II. Series.
PS3563.A4Z498   1993
813'.54—dc20   92-27568
                                                  CIP

10 9 8 7 6 5 4 3 2 1

For my children,
Elise, David, and Dorian

Contents

Preface

Bernard Malamud is one of the major American writers of the post–World War II period. *The Assistant*, which he published in 1957, has become a minor classic. Although much of his work has a Jewish content, a substantial amount does not, and Malamud resisted being called a Jewish-American Writer. He felt the title to be reductive, given the fact that his message was a universal one. It must be stressed, however, that Jews and Jewish history, culture, and religion are centrally important in his exploration of some of the basic issues facing all human beings. These issues include the importance of a correct understanding of human suffering, identifying the true nature of the human condition, and the responsibility that one human being has for another. He was also concerned with exploring the nature of art and the artistic process, sometimes within the context of Jewish themes and sometimes not.

This study consists of a close analysis of Malamud's fiction—the novels in chronological order and his short stories—and will show the development of his skill and the ways he chose to illustrate his themes. It is part of Twayne Publishers' series subtitled, "Revisited." In the earlier Twayne volume entitled *Bernard Malamud*, Sidney Richman wrote, "It seemed clear before much work was done that no *definitive* statement could be made about Malamud's first work until his last had been done."[1] The purpose of this volume is to address the problem identified by Richman in a monograph published in 1966, when less than half of Malamud's works had been written. With his unfortunate death in 1986, it is now possible to evaluate Malamud's literary vision in relation to his work as a whole and to take account of more recent scholarship. I hope that this study does justice to these goals.

Chronology

1914   Bernard Malamud born on 26 April in Brooklyn, New York, to Max and Bertha Fidelman Malamud.

1929   Mother dies at age 44.

1932   Graduates from Erasmus Hall High School.

1936   Graduates with bachelor's degree from the City College of New York.

1940   Clerk in the Bureau of the Census, Washington, D.C.

1941   Begins to write short stories.

1942   Receives master's degree from Columbia University; thesis on Thomas Hardy's *The Dynasts*.

1943   First stories published: "Benefit Performance" and "The Place Is Different Now."

1945   Marries Ann de Chiara; lives in Greenwich Village.

1947   Birth of son Paul.

1949   Completes nine years of teaching evening classes at Erasmus Hall and Harlem High Schools.

1949   Joins the English Department of Oregon State College, Corvallis; stays 12 years, rising to the rank of Associate Professor.

1950   Stories appear in *Harper's Bazaar, Partisan Review, Commentary*.

1952   *The Natural*. Birth of daughter Janna.

1956   Receives *Partisan Review* fellowship in fiction. Lives in Rome; travels in Europe.

1957   *The Assistant*.

1958   *The Magic Barrel*. *The Assistant* receives the Rosenthal Foundation Award of the National Institute of Arts and Letters and the Daroff Memorial Fiction Award of the Jewish Book Council of America. Receives Rockefeller grant.

1959   National Book Award for *The Magic Barrel*. Ford Foundation Fellowship in humanities and arts.

1961   *A New Life*. Joins the faculty of Bennington College, Bennington, Vermont.

1963   *Idiots First.* Travels in England and Italy. Awarded *Playboy Magazine*'s annual fiction prize for "Naked Nude."

1964   Member of National Institute of Arts and Letters.

1965   Travels in the Soviet Union, France, and Spain.

1966   *The Fixer.* Begins two years as a visiting lecturer at Harvard University.

1967   Member of American Academy of Arts and Sciences. *The Fixer* receives National Book Award for Fiction and a Pulitzer Prize in literature. Film version of *The Fixer.*

1968   Travels to Israel in March.

1969   *Pictures of Fidelman: An Exhibition.*

1971   *The Tenants.*

1973   *Rembrandt's Hat.*

1976   Receives Jewish Heritage Award of B'nai B'rith.

1979   *Dubin's Lives.* President of American P.E.N. Receives Governor's Award of the Vermont Council on the Arts.

1981   Receives Creative Arts Award for Fiction from Brandeis University. Fellow of the Center for Advanced Study in the Behavioral Sciences.

1982   *God's Grace.*

1983   *The Stories of Bernard Malamud.* Awarded Gold Medal for Fiction from the American Academy of Arts and Letters. Undergoes bypass surgery.

1985   Receives the Premio Mondello, a major Italian award.

1986   Malamud dies on 18 March, in New York City.

1989   *The People and Uncollected Stories* published posthumously.

Chapter One
Growing Up in Brooklyn

Bernard Malamud was born and raised in Brooklyn, New York, the son of Russian-Jewish immigrants. His mother died when he was 14 years old, and he and his younger brother were raised by their father, who worked long hours running a small grocery. Malamud has said, "Their world taught me their values. . . . The welfare of human beings, what makes a man function as a man. Theirs was a person-centered world, one that regarded the qualities of people. When I think of my father, I'm filled with a sense of sweet humanity."[1]

Throughout Malamud's writing there is a clear humanistic orientation, a concern not with worldly success but with more abstract human values—love in particular. He greatly admires selflessness and, in particular, the process of inner change and growth that can lead an individual from a limited perspective of total concern with self to one that sees the importance of that self as part of the human condition. Frequently, failure in the world in terms of acceptance and material success is seen as the prerequisite for inner, moral success. While one cannot assume that it was Malamud's background and the influence of his parents that led directly to his later humanistic attitudes, there probably were at least some influences from this "person-centered world" of his youth that made him feel that the American ideal of material achievement was inadequate, that it did not create moral individuals.

He spoke of himself as "a real child of the Depression."[2] During that period, he had to work in the census office and in a factory that manufactured yarn, to help support his financially strapped family, and he frequently deprives his characters of physical comfort, emotional well-being, freedom, or the achievement of their life's goals. He pushes them down to bedrock in order to test them, to make them come to grips with what he feels to be the centrally important facets of life—selflessness and love.

The Question of Jewish-American Authorship

Malamud has usually been referred to as a Jewish-American writer. It is not a term he relished. He protested: "I'm an American, I'm a Jew, and

I write for all men. A novelist has to or he's built himself a cage. I write about Jews, when I write about Jews, because they set my imagination going. . . . Sometimes I make characters Jewish because I think I will understand them better as people, not because I am out to prove anything. . . . I was born in America and respond in American life to more than Jewish experience. I wrote for those who read."[3] He drew attention to the fact that both Saul Bellow and Philip Roth have also resisted being labeled Jewish-American writers: "Bellow pokes fun at this sort of thing by calling 'Bellow-Malamud-Roth' the Hart, Schaffner and Marx of Jewish-American literature."[4] Even such an apparently "Jewish" author as Chaim Potok disliked being given this title.

The basic reason for Malamud's and these other author's resistance to being classified in this way has to do with their feeling that they are being underrated as writers concerned with the human condition when they are assumed to be interested in only a subgroup of humanity. Malamud—and Bellow and Roth—are certainly concerned with more than just one narrow group of people. Malamud's work shows, and he has stated categorically, that his concern is with humanity and not with Jews alone: "I handle the Jew as a symbol of the tragic experience of man existentially. I try to see the Jew as universal man. Every man is a Jew though he may not know it. The Jewish drama is a . . . symbol of the fight for existence in the highest possible human terms. Jewish history is God's gift of drama."[5]

Malamud's comment that "Every man is a Jew though he may not know it" has led to a great amount of discussion concerning the underlying meanings in his fiction. He has seen his statement as "indicating how history, sooner or later, treats all men" (Field, 11). Thus, the Jews can be seen as exemplars of the injustices that eventually affect all human beings. However, there is more to his use of Jews than this. Malamud presents them as Everyman in his attempt to cope with the pressures, human demands, and responsibilities of life. He also sees suffering as something that all humans must face; what they do with it determines the persons they become.

One critic has written that Malamud's "definition of Jewishness includes such universal human virtues as moral obligation to one's fellow man and the community; acceptance of responsibility; being involved in the suffering of others; and learning from one's own suffering."[6] Malamud certainly does use Jewishness in these ways, and one must question whether he is convincing when he gives to Jews such wide-ranging meaning. Can a single group validly depict the psychic and moral anxieties of twentieth-century men and women? Do Jews possess the moral stature for this, and can their problems and difficulties be transferred to non-Jews?

Malamud felt that his writing was universal and that "anyone sensitive to fiction can understand my work and *feel* it."[7] It is not necessary for a reader to be Jewish or of any particular race or nationality to grasp the subtleties in the writing of a good author, even if that author focuses on a small and perhaps esoteric group. This argument would apply to the writing of African-American authors such as James Baldwin and Ralph Ellison, or to William Faulkner in his treatment of the rural South. It also relates to Malamud's not being considered merely a Jewish writer: "He is a Jewish writer in the same sense that Dickens is a social-protest writer, or Jane Austen a domestic novelist."[8] His attitude toward Jews and humanity may be briefly stated as being that "the Jew is humanity under the twin aspects of suffering and moral aspiration. Therefore any man who suffers greatly and also longs to be better than he is, can be called a Jew."[9]

I have been addressing the question of whether Malamud's treatment of Jews permits them to represent all humanity. But what of the effect on Jews and Jewish history of this attempt to expand their meaning to encompass so much? Is there a distortion—perhaps even a demeaning—of Jews and Jewish history, or are certain aspects of modern Jewish experience ignored because they do not easily fit into a more universal set of implications?

While Malamud does present particular aspects of Jewish belief, history, and culture in *The Fixer, God's Grace,* and in many of his short stories, these are usually only the means to an end, giving his fiction what Isaac Bashevis Singer calls "an address." In his novel *The Tenants,* Malamud deals with a problem directly relevant to Jews in modern America: the black-Jewish conflict of the late 1960s, but even in that book, the protagonist Harry Lesser is Jewish by birth only; he does not show any attachment to Judaism or to Jewish culture. Rather than representing Jews or, in his case, even all men, Lesser shows forth aspects of the artist and his problems with the dichotomy of art and life. He can provide a jumping-off point for an investigation of the problems of black-Jewish relations in contemporary America, as can the landlord Levenspiel, if one simply accepts him as Jewish, and does not ask what sort of Jew he is, what Judaism means to him, or whether he shows any signs of feeling some relation to Jewish history. He calls himself a Jew, and that seems to be sufficient for Malamud.

In commenting on critic Leslie Fiedler's tendency "to see everything, including American literature, in Jewish terms," another critic remarks that "Fiedler's point in re-Judaizing Malamud is that Malamud, like other contemporary Jewish-American writers, is de-Judaizing his material."[10] It might be argued that Malamud is "de-Judaizing" his work through the paucity of connection to and understanding of things Jewish on the part of those characters who are supposed to be Jews. Yet the overtones of Jewish history and its "drama" remain, to add depth to many of the short stories and to novels like *The Assistant,* parts of *Pictures of Fidelman,* and *The Tenants.*

Philip Roth has had reservations concerning Malamud's orientation both to the contemporary world and to his use of Jews as metaphors. Roth writes:

The Jews of *The Magic Barrel* and the Jews of *The Assistant* are not the Jews of New York or Chicago. They are Malamud's invention, a metaphor of sorts to stand for certain possibilities and promises, and I am further inclined to believe this when I read the statement attributed to Malamud which goes, 'All men are Jews.' In fact, we know this is not so; even the men who are Jews aren't sure they're Jews. But Malamud as a writer of fiction has not shown specific interest in the anxieties and dilemmas and corruptions of the contemporary American Jew, the Jew we think of as characteristic of our times.[11]

This is from an early essay (1961) that could not take into account books like *The Tenants* or *Rembrandt's Hat,* both of which are more concerned with the contemporary Jew. However, Roth clearly believes that Malamud is using Jews in ways that are problematic. In the texts Roth mentions, Malamud is concerned, as Roth later states in the same article, with "what it is to be human, and to be humane . . . (Roth 1975, 127). Malamud's Jews are timeless, and his remark that "all men are Jews" must be seen in this timeless sense and not in the more limited manner which Roth's remarks imply. I would agree with Jeffrey Helterman's observation: "While Malamud does not have the intellectual range of Bellow or command of Roth's verbal pyrotechnics, his moral vision reaches depths unprobed by either of his peers."[12]

Malamud does not populate his fiction with Jews alone. Italian Catholics comprise the second largest ethnic group in his writing. His marriage to Ann de Chiara in 1945 both greatly expanded his experience with a non-Jewish group and, interestingly, made him think more deeply about his Jewishness. He said, "Another thing that has caused me to be concerned with Jewish subject matter is the fact that I'm married to a Gentile. This made me ask myself what it is I'm entitled to in Jewish experience."[13] The effects of this are clear in many of the short stories and in *Pictures of Fidelman*. I feel, however, that Malamud's tales concerning Jews have more depth than those that place Italian characters at their center. This has to do with the sense of history and suffering that suffuses the "Jewish" tales, the characters frequently carrying this history along with them, sometimes despite themselves.

Malamud was greatly affected by World War II. He was not particularly concerned about his own Jewishness until the events of the Holocaust, and said, "The rise of totalitarianism, the Second World War, and the situation of the Jews in Europe helped me to come to what I wanted to say as a writer."[14] He became convinced that he wanted to be a writer and began a study of Jewish history and culture. In 1958, in the early years of his career when he was beginning to attract attention, he said that "the purpose of the writer . . . is to keep civilization from destroying itself" (Field 1975, 7). Although he does not stint in his presentation of the difficulties of existence for his characters, until *The Tenants* his underlying view in his novels, though less so in the short stories, leans strongly toward the possibility of human betterment. In the latter half of his writing career, Malamud's work shows a more pessimistic cast.

Despite a growing tendency toward pessimism, one which is not so sanguine concerning the individual's ability to tap reserves of compassion and charity, Malamud maintained faith in the human spirit. As late as 1979, he said he felt that it might be possible to change human beings, and that this was one goal he sought to achieve: "I want my writing ultimately to be moving. If you move someone, there's the possibility he may change. . . . The more I experience life, the more I become aware of illusion as primary experience."[15]

This later attitude, a mixture of the positive and negative—some might say a more realistic view of the human condition—is summed up in a remark Malamud made in an interview, also in 1979: "I have a tragic sense of life . . . but it's a source of stability, security. You're not kidding yourself. If you have a sense of where the darkness is, you also know where the light is. Life is a tragedy full of joy" (Lask, 43). Like Faulkner, Malamud sees humankind as enduring, despite his recognition of the difficulties of life and human limitations. He is not a pie-in-the-sky optimist but rather a writer who believes that the human spirit may be capable of overcoming the pressures in modern civilization that would destroy it.

Malamud saw himself as an American writer who writes for all people. He was influenced more by non-Jewish American and European authors than by Jewish ones: " . . . as a writer, I've been influenced by Hawthorne, James, Mark Twain, Hemingway, more than I have by Sholem Aleichem and I. L. Peretz."[16] He felt that the influences of the Yiddish language on his writing have been over stressed, and said, "What I actually do best is what I call immigrant English."[17] Although his parents spoke Yiddish, he never spoke it himself with facility but learned to understand it. His prose does possess the "quality of Yiddish," largely because of his use of certain idioms and an unconventional word order that "might derive as much from Latin or German as from Yiddish" (Tyler, 33).

American and Other Literary Influences

An American author with whom Malamud shares many thematic concerns is Nathaniel Hawthorne. Jackson Benson observes that both authors

possess the ability to combine with great skill, reality and the dream, the natural and supernatural. That dream-reality mixture so powerful in Malamud stories such as "Idiots First," "The Silver Crown," or "The Magic Barrel" may owe more to Hawthorne stories like "My Kinsman Major Molineux," "Young Goodman Brown," and "The Birthmark" than to Kafka, who is so frequently cited in this regard as a model. Malamud also shares with Hawthorne certain other modes and subjects, such as the "mysterious stranger," the "ghostly search," the "test of faith," the "peculiar mark of habit," and perhaps most importantly, that theme of Hawthorne's "Ethan Brand" which could be called "hardness of heart." (Benson, 17)

While Malamud cannot be said to be concerned with secret sin in all human beings, as is Hawthorne, he shares Hawthorne's belief that for an individual to grow morally he must be honest with himself in confronting those flaws that prevent him from being open and truthful with his fellows. In both authors' work these flaws create characters who are self-centered and cut off from others. Through experience with life, suffering, and introspection, Malamud's characters frequently can overcome their apartness from the human race and reach a point of selflessness and an understanding of the difficulties faced by all human beings.

Hawthorne is more pessimistic than Malamud in this area, as he rarely permits his isolated characters to reach the understanding necessary for full integration with society or with other individuals. While there are in certain of Malamud's novels and short stories the element of darkness and "weight" that is so common in Hawthorne's work, Malamud, unlike Hawthorne, frequently relieves this aura with a wry humor that Hawthorne lacks. Malamud has said that he "was very much influenced by Charlie Chaplin's movies . . . by the rhythm and snap of his comedy and his wonderful, wonderful mixture of comedy and sadness—one of his major gifts that I've studied with great care" (Tyler, 33). This use of comedy, which is often prominent in the presentation of what might be called his moral fables, permits Malamud to attain the bittersweet quality that marks so much of his fiction and that is lacking in Hawthorne's writing. The ambiguity of many of the characterizations and endings of Malamud's works parallels Hawthorne's use of the same device but contains this wry undercurrent of humor that gives it its distinctiveness.

Shades of Henry James can also be seen. Like James, Malamud is concerned with the underlying causes of human actions and the nuances of understanding that pass between characters. He is not as subtle as James in his presentation of character interaction but, like him, is very concerned with form, a discussion of which occurs throughout *The Tenants,* wherein the protagonist, Harry Lesser, is a novelist for whom Jamesian subtlety is a primary goal. In many short stories, particularly those with an Italian setting, the influence of James's international theme can be seen. *Pictures of Fidelman* depicts this in the protagonist's role as a naive American responding to the Italian scene, and in Fidelman's concern with the nature of art, Malamud uses another Jamesian theme.

Malamud has said that "with me it's story, story, story" (Shenker, 22). In both his orientation to story and to dialect, Mark Twain is an author whom Malamud admires. Malamud's use in various works of immigrant English, Yiddish inflections, American black English, and white slang places him within the oral tradition for which Twain is well known. His use of humor to heighten the effectiveness of his presentation of moral issues also parallels Twain's in its reliance upon irony. In addition, both share a concern with the survival of innocence in a corrupt world. His concern with story also has attracted him to Hemingway, but Hemingway's influence has been primarily in the area of style. Malamud has said he believes "it is to Hemingway more than Yiddish that he owes his ability to compress" (Tyler, 33).

Also to be seen in Malamud's writing is the idea of salvation through suffering, which is developed in the work of Dostoyevski, and what Samuel Bluefarb has called "the surrealistic mode of a James Joyce—a technique which the later Fidelman stories exemplify."[18] This surrealism is also present in parts of *The Tenants* and in a number of short stories. Finally, there are parallels with the work of Franz Kafka. Joel Salzberg quotes Neil Rudin's observation that "Kafka and Malamud share the same concerns in their depiction of the misery and mystery of life, that both are anchored to the Yiddish literary tradition, and that they ultimately affirm love and responsibility as the only means of surviving in an inscrutable world."[19] While shared thematic concerns certainly can be seen between Malamud and Kafka, except in those works in which Malamud opts for a surrealistic style the method of presentation of those themes is quite different in the two authors.

The issues and themes discussed in this chapter will reappear in discussions of the fiction, to be treated at length in relation to specific works. The background material included here makes its presence felt throughout Malamud's writing, particularly after the fist novel, *The Natural*. It is with that novel that this study begins.

Chapter Two
The Natural

Legends and Women

Malamud's first novel is a strange amalgam of fact and fable, the mundane and fantasy. It concerns a character who wants to be the best baseball player ever and who possesses very special heroic qualities. Unfortunately, Roy Hobbs does not possess the vision necessary to see beyond his goal of breaking baseball records, which in Malamud's view means that he is interested only in self-aggrandizement and not in serving humanity. In Malamud's fiction, self-centeredness is always a primal sin that is severely punished until the individual changes his attitude.

The mythological is central to *The Natural* (1952),[1] and I think it is best viewed from the vantage point of the three women that Malamud presents to the protagonist, as each carries with her certain aspects of the myths and legends relevant to Roy Hobbs's situation. Indeed, it is Roy's response to Harriet Bird, Memo Paris, and Iris Lemon that permits us to gauge his character.

Harriet Bird enters Roy's train at a "desolate station" and proceeds to drop a rose, which Roy retrieves for her. This innocent introduction does not prepare us for the later realization that Harriet is a murderess of the avenging angel variety. After watching Roy strike out Whammer Wambold in a trackside contest, she introduces the legendary overtones of the event into the novel. Roy sees her as "a girl on horseback—reviewing the inspiring sight (she said it was) of David jawboning the Goliath-Whammer, or was it Sir Percy lancing Sir Maldemer, or the first son (with a rock in his paw) ranged against the primitive papa?"[2] She refers to the contest as a "tourney," and Roy thinks of her as "a snappy goddess." The combination of biblical and Arthurian allusions is Malamud's first attempt to raise the novel's events to a mythic level. A central issue for the reader, however, is whether baseball, despite its important position as an American ritual, can carry the weight of allusion that Malamud places upon it. Is the game simply too lightweight to become

9

the foundation for biblical, Arthurian, fertility, Grail, and hero and kingship myths? I think Malamud strains credulity at times, as we shall see.

Harriet exposes the limitation in Roy's personality: ability without vision is not enough. She asks him if he has read Homer, and all he can think about is "four bases and not a book" (*TN,* 34). She attempts to stretch his concept of his role as a future hero to include a sense of the importance of heroes to the human race. Because of her difficulty in explaining it, perhaps Roy can be forgiven for not understanding what Harriet wants, but it is clear that he has no goals other than those that will feed his personal vanity. As Earl Wasserman points out, "It is the infantilism of the American hero that Malamud is concerned with, the psychic and therefore moral regression of the gifted 'natural' who could vitalize society and reveal to it the capacities of human strength . . ." (Wasserman, 446). It is to the American hero, but also to the hero in his wider implications as a mythological figure that Malamud is alluding. Because of his attachment to the peculiarly American game of baseball, Roy does retain a clearly American aspect, however, and becomes, in Frederick Turner's phrase, "the prototypical goon athlete . . ." (Turner, 114), someone whose lack of depth and weight cannot carry the overtones of meaning that Malamud desires.

It seems likely that Malamud himself recognized the need to add a further dimension to baseball because it was too light an area around which to center a serious novel. In 1986 he stated, "Baseball had interested me, especially its comic aspects, but I wasn't able to write about the game until I transformed game into myth, via Jessie Weston's Percival legend with an assist by T. S. Eliot's 'The Waste Land' plus the lives of several ball players I had read, in particular Babe Ruth's and Bobby Feller's. The myth enriched the baseball lore as feats of magic transformed the game."[3] Malamud may well have felt that the enriching of baseball lore was a necessity.

Upon realizing that Roy will replace the Whammer as a major heroic figure, Harriet switches her attentions to Roy, and shoots him in a ritualistic manner. She uses a silver bullet, which alludes ironically to the justice-dealing Lone Ranger and, as one critic observes, to Mickey Spillane.[4] She then, "making muted noises of triumph and despair, danced on her toes around the stricken hero" (*TN,* 43). The implication here is that her triumph lies in stopping the advance of an unworthy hero; her despair, in the fact that he is one. Another view of this scene is that she is simply destructive; Malamud's references to the pain caused her when Roy touches her breast and to her being a "twisted tree" (*TN,* 37) heighten this possibility, particularly as he uses references to "sick" breasts (Memo has one too) to represent sterility. Also, as Jeffrey Helterman remarks, "Throughout the novel, birds symbolize the force of the destructive mother archetype" (Helterman 1978, 292). Harriet may best be viewed as representative of fate, the force that will not permit the fulfillment of what individuals desire but controls what must be. In Roy's case, it is on account of his assuredness and lack of humility, as well as his self-centeredness and lack of a wider sense of responsibility, that he is brought down.

After shooting Roy, Harriet disappears, though not entirely. It is an accurate observation that her "presence broods over the entire novel. As one who will destroy a hero rather than have him waste his gifts, she is the spiritual ancestor of the two women who will be rivals for Roy's love. For this reason, Malamud puts the symbols for both women—white roses for Iris, the hero-nurturer, and a black-feathered hat for Memo, the hero-destroyer—in Harriet's hotel room."[5] After Harriet, the next important woman that Roy meets is Memo Paris, who takes on Harriet's chastizing role, but for very different reasons.

Memo Paris is Pop Fisher's niece and Bump Bailey's mistress. This links her to both the ailing Fisher King (Pop) and the failed hero (Bump). Although Pop is attached to nature and feels that he should have been a farmer, his ability to make things grow, his "green thumb," has lost its power: "It's been a blasted dry season. No rains at all. The grass is worn scabby in the outfield and the infield is cracking" (*TN,* 47). Even the water fountain does not work properly. A further sign of his impotence, his inability to act, is the athlete's foot on his hands. He is waiting for someone or something to rescue him and his lackluster team, the Knights, from the oblivion into which both are slipping. Bump is a great batter but has no sense of responsibility toward the team, being interested only in his own prowess and glory; he does not inspire his teammates to greater efforts and does not, therefore, fulfill the hero's role. That Memo is attached to Bump and Pop foreshadows the negative role she will play in Roy's life, that of destructive seductress who desires to destroy the hero not because he does not live up to the qualities of the heroes of legend but out of revenge and an inherent sterility in her nature.

Memo has the already mentioned "sick breast" and is depicted as leading Roy to a stream next to which is a sign reading DANGER. POLLUTED WATER. Roy's task in terms of fertility myths is to bring water to Pop and the team, thus revitalizing the Knights, curing the

Fisher King's ailment, and restoring fertility to the field ("Knights' Field"). Memo Paris's role (that of Morgan le Fay) is to prevent this by testing the hero and causing him to fail. When Roy is in his slump, Memo loses interest in him, her task apparently accomplished. She still blames him for Bump's death but as Bump was not in the true heroic mold, there was no possibility of his rejuvenating the team; for Memo, Roy may pose a more serious threat. When there is the chance that Roy will successfully lead the Knights to the pennant, Memo invites him and the rest of the team to a party the night before a very important game. She piles more and more food onto Roy's plate, but the more he eats the hungrier he becomes. He feels that he is "searching for something that he couldn't find" (*TN*, 187), and wonders, "What must I do not to be hungry?" (*TN*, 189). The knight is supposed to fast before his test, but Memo undermines Roy. One critic remarks that "Roy Hobbs is destroyed by false love, compulsively sacrificing his destiny to the desire of the moment. . . ."[6] Memo takes his weaknesses, plays upon them, and destroys him.

Nowhere are Memo's destructive qualities seen more clearly than in her alliance with the Judge and Gus Sands. She delivers the message from the Judge to Roy that will mean betrayal of the team and final destruction of Roy's hopes of greatness; she kisses him when he agrees to collude with the Judge; she has already made it clear that she will only stay with a man who has wealth. Sandy Cohen feels that "Memo reveals herself for what she really is, first as the bitch-goddess of the American Dream . . . then as the goddess of sterility and darkness; she proposes to Roy the Judge's offer to throw the playoff game in exchange for money to buy her and that American Dream."[7]

She is also a close companion of Gus Sands, the Supreme Bookie. He is a Merlin figure with an almost supernatural ability to foretell the future—that is, to win bets, to guess the outcome of unpredictable events. Even he wants assurances, however, and forms a pact with the Judge and Memo to fix the game. One critic describes Gus Sands as a "Satanic figure . . . (the august Prince of the Barren Land), who dwells in the Hellish nightclub, the Pot of Fire" (Helterman 1978, 293). The final alliance is foreshadowed halfway through the novel when Roy meets Judge Banner, Gus, and Memo at the Pot of Fire. The diabolic atmosphere and Roy's need to use magic to defeat (temporarily) the skill of Gus Sands heightens the unreality that is an inherent part of a tale rooted in the otherwise mundane world of baseball. Memo as real woman and as a Morgan le

Fay–Lilith figure plays a central part in the realistic-allegorical nature of the novel.

Even more important than Memo is Iris Lemon. Steven J. Rubin notes that "Malamud's women are often presented as either saviors or destroyers. Nowhere is this dichotomy more evident than in *The Natural*. It is Roy Hobbs's fate, however, not to be able to distinguish between the two."[8] Roy's shallowness and his lack of insight into the values held by the two women parallels his lack of insight into the heroic ideal, into what is required of the true hero. Memo is lust and the immediate gratification of the body; Iris is love and the responsibility that the gifted individual has for others. Memo is self; Iris is selflessness. "Memo is a creator of illusions, Iris is all substance" (Helterman 1985, 28). Roy understands none of this.

Iris first appears in the novel when Roy notices her in the stands, a "black-haired woman, wearing a red dress . . ." (*TN*, 145), the direct opposite of Memo, with her red hair and black dress. As Memo is the evil knight destroyer—the Morgan le Fay figure—so Iris is depicted as the benevolent knight supporter—the Lady of the Lake figure. Iris stands twice when Roy is at bat and still in his slump, as though to give a public sign of her confidence and faith in him. Roy thinks of Memo's avoiding him as soon as he went into his slump, while "Iris, a stranger, had done for him what the other wouldn't . . ." (*TN*, 153). She is not sure herself why she is concerned about just another ball player's slump, but it becomes clear that she thinks he has the ability to offer something to others. As she explains herself to Roy: "'Because I hate to see a hero fail. There are so few of them.' She said it seriously and he felt she meant it. 'Without heroes we're all plain people and don't know how far we can go'" (*TN*, 155).

It is clear from Roy's response to this that he does not know what Iris is talking about, in much the same way that he did not know what Harriet was talking about. One critic sees Iris as an "earth mother figure, Iris Lemon (both flower and fruit suggest fertility and life) . . ." (Helterman 1978, 294). Iris is a life-giving figure because she desires to bring out the best in Roy and gives of herself to do this. She recognizes that heroes must do more than just break records; they must use the power that they possess, which ordinary mortals lack, to set an example as human beings for the rest of humankind. A further exchange shows how much she understands of life and how much Roy does not:

"I wanted everything." His voice boomed out in the silence.

She waited.

"I had a lot to give to this game."

"Life?"

"Baseball." . . .

"But I don't understand why you should make so much of that. Are your values so—" (*TN*, 157)

Unfortunately, Roy's values *are* "so—." He lives within baseball and cannot see beyond it. He desires to be a baseball hero rather than a mythic, Grail hero. To become the latter would require a level of virtue and the sacrifice of his baser instincts that Roy is incapable of. The clearest sign of this incapacity is his choice of Memo over Iris. His constant hunger has been referred to, as has Memo's pressing him to eat "huge quantities of food—a counterfeit of love (the analogue of Harriet Bird's bullet)—until Roy collapses with a 'colossal belly-ache,' a re-enactment of the past . . ." (Baumbach 1963, 447). Roy realizes that Memo is "like all the food he had lately been eating, that left him, after the having of it, unsatisfied, sometimes even with a greater hunger than before" (*TN*, 167). Yet his lust for her remains undiminished.

At times he dreams of a home and a child, with Memo cast in the role of wife and mother, making home-cooked meals and waiting for him to return. He realizes, however, that "the picture he had drawn of Memo sitting domestically home wasn't exactly the girl she was. The kind he had in mind, though it bothered him to admit it, was more like Iris seemed to be, only she didn't suit him" (*TN*, 181). She does not suit him because she demands responsibility and she is a grandmother; that would make him a grandfather, and he is too egotistical to be able to accept that. "Ironically, he must learn to choose the real before he can become the mythic hero he embodies" (Goldman, 163).

Roy's ability to be the hero is reflected in the condition of his bat, which he has named Wonderboy. Roy made the bat from a lightning-struck tree, and the bat is "like a leg bone" (*TN*, 76), an allusion to biblical references to the sacrifice of thigh bones to Jehovah. There are also parallels to Excalibur and its magical qualities, and to the lance of a medieval knight in the pitcher Vogelman's description of Roy at bat: "He looked again and saw Roy, in full armor, mounted on a black charger. . . . Yes, there he was coming at him with a long lance as thick as a young tree" (*TN*, 232). The "young tree" is one of many references to the phallic symbolism carried by the bat. The power, the fertility of Wonderboy is dependent upon Roy's state of mind, or his soul. During his slump, "Wonderboy resembled a sagging baloney" (*TN*, 148). But Roy's loyalty to the bat as magic wand and amulet is rewarded by a home run and by his saving the life of the boy who had placed his faith in him. Iris's faith in Roy, shown by her standing up, is an important factor in Roy's coming out of his slump and regaining his potency; but even when Roy becomes the savior of the Knights he refuses to accept her.

As Excalibur and phallic symbol, Wonderboy both introduces and ends Roy's trial as hero. In their first time at bat for the Knights in an actual game, Roy and Wonderboy knock the cover off the ball. Immediately it begins raining and continues to rain for three days. The grass grows, and the drought is over. The Knights have new life, and Pop's athlete's foot of the hands is cured. So long as Roy keeps faith with his fans, even if he is unable to reach full heroic stature, Wonderboy serves him well. After he drives off with Memo, thinks she has hit a boy but can find nothing, and proceeds to crash the car himself, his slump begins and the Knights begin to fade. He has given himself to Memo and what she represents—corruption and the anti-heroic.

At the end of the novel, after Roy has agreed to help the Knights lose, Wonderboy again reacts, splitting in half as though to stress Roy's impurity. In a scene depicting Roy's ritualistic burial of the bat in left field, he wonders "if the bat had willed its own brokenness . . ." (*TN*, 235). He even considers watering the ground where he has buried it in the hope that "it would take root and become a tree" (*TN*, 235). Without Wonderboy, Roy is finished as a baseball player; without his sword, his lance, his fertility object, he cannot conquer. Malamud's combining of the search for the Grail (the pennant) with fertility myths and the plight of the failed Arthurian hero creates the complexity of the novel. As Wasserman observes, Roy is shot in spring, joins the Knights in summer, and with his "failure in the last crucial game the novel ends in a wintry autumn to complete the fertility cycle inherent in both the Grail Quest and the schedule of the baseball season" (Wasserman, 442).

In keeping with the mythical death and resurrection of the hero, Malamud has a 20-year-old pitcher, who wants to be a farmer, pitch to Roy at a crucial point in the last game. Herman Youngberry strikes Roy out as Roy had previously struck out Whammer Wambold, to replace him as the putative hero. Alluding to the treatment meted out to failed heroes who do not provide the masses with the nourishment they expect, Roy fears that "the mob would swarm all over him, tear him apart, and strew his polluted remains over the field . . ." (TN, 234). The final statement of failure, which one fan makes to another is, "He coulda been a king . . ." (TN, 237). Roy's ideas of kingship were too limited. As Jonathan Baumbach remarks, "A romantic, Malamud writes of heroes; a realist, he writes of their defeats" (Baumbach 1963, 439).

Suffering and Growth

In *The Natural,* Malamud uses a theme that will appear in all of his novels and most of his stories: suffering as a possible means to moral growth. I say "possible" because whether growth will take place depends on the attitude of the character. In Roy's case, little is learned, his differences from Iris stressing his inability to understand what can be learned from suffering:

> "Experience makes good people better."
>
> She was staring at the lake.
>
> "How does it do that?"
>
> "Through their suffering."
>
> "I had enough of that," he said in disgust.
>
> "We have two lives, Roy, the life we learn with and the life we live with after that. Suffering is what brings us toward happiness." . . .
>
> "It teaches us to want the right things."
>
> "All it taught me is to stay away from it. I am sick of all I have suffered."
>
> She shrank away a little. (TN, 159)

His attitude indicates that Roy's moral development is very limited, although a change does occur toward the end of the novel, when it is too late. Despite the lack of major change during the course of the novel, Malamud concentrates on the suffering Roy endures, his responses to it, and his lack of understanding of the selflessness required of him. When Malamud was asked about his attitude toward suffering in his work, he replied: "I'm against it but when it occurs why waste the experience?" (Stern, 55). This somewhat amusing response should not be taken to show that Malamud takes suffering lightly; indeed, he takes it most seriously and uses it as a means to characterize his protagonists.

As in most of Malamud's works, the present can be understood only by appreciating the effects of the past. Roy is obsessed with the past, in particular with his youth. One of the constant threads in Roy's personality is his desire to regain the innocence of childhood. On the first page we are told that Roy has no "timepiece"; later, he will hit a ball into the ball park clock and smash it. He desires to stop time or deny its existence so as to return to the period before Harriet Bird shot him and to live again in unsullied hope, and he must go even further back, to the period before his days in the orphanage, to the time when he lived with his grandmother. He is always trying to run away from events in his past that do not permit him to see the world in terms of simplicity and purity. Of course he cannot escape from those events, and his attempts to do so show that he has not learned from them. He remembers "how satisfied he had been as a youngster, . . . and he wished he could have lived longer in his boyhood" (*TN,* 119).

Roy's obsession with the past comes to a head in a surrealistic scene in which he fantasizes that Memo destroys his youth, with its dreams and innocence. Memo is driving at night without lights, and Roy thinks he sees a boy and his dog on the country road on which they are speeding. He is sure that Memo has hit the boy, but she says no:

> He reached for the brake.
>
> "Don't, it was just something on the road."
>
> "I heard somebody groan."
>
> "That was yourself." (*TN,* 125)

Roy cannot recall his groaning, but when he returns to search for the body, there is nothing there. As in *The Great Gatsby,* the protagonist does not see that the woman to whom he is attracted is corrupt. Even when Memo, like Daisy, refuses to stop the car, Roy is still besotted with her. There are other parallels between Roy and Gatsby, the most important being that they desire to recover an idealized period from their past—an impossibility for both.

In *The Natural,* Malamud begins the theme of fatherhood, which will be of central importance in his writing. It is important for the process of salvation, which requires movement from selfishness to selflessness and acceptance of responsibility for others. The movement from lover to father is one that Roy Hobbs makes far too late, only after he hits Iris with the ball and she tells him that she is pregnant with his child. Roy can then accept her being a grandmother and his being a father.

Fatherhood causes Roy much suffering. Early in the novel, he tells us that sometimes he had wanted to "skull" his own father, who, after the death of Roy's grandmother, had "dumped me in one orphan home after the other, wherever he happened to be working—when he did . . ." (*TN*, 34). He then accidentally causes the death of Sam Simpson— clearly a substitute father whom he loves—who sees in Roy the fulfillment of dreams of success that he was unable to achieve himself. In the trackside contest, Roy not only hits Sam with a very fast ball that injures him fatally, but he also strikes out Whammer Wambold, thus fulfilling the myth that requires the new hero to destroy and replace the old. Whammer is no father figure; nor is Bump Baily, who because of Roy's influence feels it necessary to go after a fly ball that forces him into the outfield wall, killing him. Both, however, are players that Roy must replace as a hero figure. It is Sam Simpson and, most important, Pop Fisher, who are the father figures in the novel.

As previously noted, Pop is the Fisher King trying to lead the Knights to success in their quest for the pennant. Pop is ethical and selfless in his support of the team, but he requires a hero to revitalize it and sees in Roy the qualities the team so desperately needs. Although Roy recognizes Pop's role as his father in a spiritual sense, he chooses Memo over him, just as he chooses her over Iris. Roy's shortsightedness is again apparent, and the suffering that it causes leads too late to his reformation, preceeded as it is by his disloyal and treacherous action in agreeing to throw the game. Not only is he unable to accept the responsibility of fatherhood himself, he acts in a way that is tantamount to destroying his spiritual father.

Unable to accept the responsibility of serving a father, Roy is also unable to take on the role himself; for Malamud, a very serious shortcoming that highlights Roy's self-centeredness. After collapsing before being able to make love to Memo, Roy is taken to a hospital with which the Judge has a special arrangement for treating the players. It is a maternity hospital. The doctors have to use a stomach pump on him, and he is delivered of "unbelievable quantities of bilge" and "moaned along with the ladies in labor on the floor . . ." (*TN*, 193). The overtones of motherhood here are more amusing than convincing; Malamud is implying that somehow Roy must learn the importance of suffering for the sake of another and realize that it cannot be avoided, so that he will contain something of more value than bilge.

One sign of growth in Roy is an image that he sees in his delirium while in the hospital: "Iris's sad head topped Memo's dancing body, with

Memo's vice versa upon the shimmying rest of Iris, a confused fusion that dizzied him. He hungered in nightmare for quantities of exotic food . . ." (*TN,* 193). While this can be seen as a continuation of his obsession with Memo, it also shows that he is beginning to see Iris as desirable and as a possible substitute for Memo. His continuing desire for love ("exotic food") is closer to realization, since that is something that Iris can fulfill. At last she becomes a central part of his subconscious; this bodes well for his future development as one who can accept the implications of human suffering—that of others and his own. As one critic has observed, ". . . what really renders Iris loathly to him is that she, unwed mother who has been associated with suffering, does not wish to bury her past but insists on bringing the memory of her shame into her present life and into Roy's."[9] Iris's motherhood, and grandmotherhood, with the implications of Roy's becoming a father, and grandfather, has been at the root of his resistance to her. While he is not yet ready for fatherhood, his hallucination is a hopeful sign, one that foreshadows his acceptance of the pregnant Iris toward the end of the novel.

Wanting to see whether he is able to bat, Roy decides to go to the ball park, and "amid a procession of fathers leaving the hospital at baby-feeding time, he sneaked out of the building" (*TN,* 196). That he is among a group of fathers does not, of course, make him a father. It provides a contrast between the state of fatherhood and his own. This is stressed when, upon his return to the hospital, we are told that "nobody had missed him" (*TN,* 196); that is, there were no mothers or babies to whom he was attached and for whom he had any responsibility. Until he commits himself to Iris at the end of the novel and is willing to take responsibility for his unborn child, he feels responsible only to himself and Wonderboy. The care and attention that he lavishes on his bat (he has "created" it himself) must be transferred to human beings. Earl Wasserman believes that "Roy's failure to be the hero is his failure to accept the mature father role . . ." (Wasserman, 459). The two are inextricably intertwined.

Roy's egocentrism has been channeled into breaking records in baseball. Toward the end of the novel, he is told by a doctor that because of his high blood pressure and athlete's heart, he will die if he plays baseball for another season. The game can no longer provide a focus for his future efforts, and although he tries to resist coming to grips with this fact, he begins thinking of alternatives—still with Memo. The doctor says that he will tell no one of Roy's state of health because he believes in "the principle of freedom of action" (*TN,* 197). The irony here is that Roy's obsession with self-aggrandizement in baseball severely limits his possible choices. Of course, this limitation is self-imposed, but its effects are real nonetheless. Life outside baseball, even with Memo, seems a blank to him. When he finally decides to try to reverse his decision to throw the game, it proves to be impossible, as it is too late. He recognizes that "I never did learn anything out of my past life, now I have to suffer again" (*TN,* 237). The final line of the novel reveals a beaten man.

Although at the close of the novel Roy has grown to the extent that he chooses Iris over Memo, accepts the responsibility of fatherhood, and recognizes the importance of love, Malamud does not permit him the salvation that will often be awarded to his later protagonists who show this kind of growth. Roy has finally seen the importance and truth in Iris's understanding of human relations and of what can be learned through suffering. Despite this, Malamud seems to feel that it took too long for enlightenment to be reached and that Roy's past sufferings have not taught him enough. Given his final change, this negative ending seems unwarranted, particularly when Roy is compared to the protagonists of *The Tenants,* who also end disastrously but who have learned nothing about selflessness and human responsibility. Perhaps this ending is best viewed as the negative aspect of the ambiguous conclusions that will follow. They will frequently show a guarded optimism, qualified by the burdens of responsibility and love. The conclusion of *The Natural* shows that Malamud was not yet ready to assert that salvation is achieved through suffering, responsibility, and love freely given.

Form and Content

One critic has observed of *The Natural:* "Moreover, the style imposes on the novel a sense of unreality which in itself suspends disbelief in much the same fashion a fairy tale does."[10] This sense of unreality is not total, since Malamud moves the narrative from fantasy and myth to the solidity of a baseball team's locker room. What happens on the diamond is also frequently nothing more than the mundane process of a struggling team's attempts to play baseball well enough to justify its existence. The "fairy tale" aspect enters with the realization that the ground has shifted and the tale is no longer about a baseball game but about mythic contests and heroic struggles. This combination of reality and unreality detracts from both. Sandy Cohen thinks that "the action works brilliantly on the mythic level . . . ," a point with which I disagree, as baseball cannot support the mythic structure. Cohen goes on to state that "on the human level it is hopelessly improbable" because "over-reliance upon myth tends to reduce the characters to mere functionaries. . . . If the protagonists of *The Natural* were to remove their masks we would discover that there is nothing behind them" (Cohen, 29–30). This is a sounder observation, as the weight of the mythic structure serves to obfuscate the more naturally human aspects of the characters and to lead the tale into odd and somewhat implausible areas, such as those discussed in the first section of this chapter.

Unlike Malamud's later novels, *The Natural* contains no Jewish characters. Robert Alter thinks that this fact helps explain why "the underpinnings of reality are finally pulled away by the powerful tug of fantasy."[11] The Jewish characters in a number of the short stories published in *The Magic Barrel* and *Idiots First* (Alter's observation was made in 1966) do not show strong "underpinnings of reality." However, it may be argued that, following *The Natural*, the three novels that were published in 1966 or earlier—*The Assistant, A New Life,* and *The Fixer*— all show a strong tie to the difficulties of the everyday on the part of their Jewish protagonists. None of them attempts excursions into legend and fantasy, so a direct comparison cannot be made. It can be seen, though, that the Jewish roots of Morris Bober, Seymour Levin, and Yakov Bok do not permit a drift away from reality, despite some elements of fantasy in *The Assistant.* Even in *God's Grace,* Malamud's last completed novel, which is based on an utterly fantastic situation, Calvin Cohn tries to impose a Jewish worldview upon the apes that share his world. Cohn will not accept the fabulous nature of his situation but must attempt the creation of a moral reality based on the solidity of Judaism.

In *The Natural,* there is a problem with the overall tone because of the shifts from seriousness to comedy and myth to reality. Robert Ducharme comments that "one does not know whether he is reading a serio-comic novel (for despite its humor, the book's theme and many of its events are quite serious in nature) or a mock-epic in prose. . . . The entire mythic undergirding becomes a toy in Malamud's hands" (Ducharme, 34–35). These shifts play havoc with the reader's expectations. Should the novel be read totally as an allegory? Can characters like Whammer Wambold, Bump Bailey, or Roy himself be presented as lightweight or comic in one scene, yet be expected to carry serious mythological weight in the next? Ducharme goes on to state: "When the novel ends on a serious note, it seems inappropriate to the pervasively comic tone. . . . To draw parallels between Roy, a virtual buffoon, and Sir Percival or Achilles is absurd if done seriously. If done ironically, the effect is to diminish the image of Roy as hero to the level of mockery" (Ducharme, 35–36). Because these extreme qualities pervade the novel, Wasserman is correct in describing it as a mixture of "Ring Lardner and Jung" (Wasserman, 440).

Despite the numerous allusions to Western and universal myths, *The Natural* is very much in the American grain, on account of its reliance on the national sport and its actual events and players (Eddie Waitkus, Babe Ruth, Shoeless Joe Jackson), metaphorical though this reliance often is. Malamud said: "I love metaphor. It provides two loaves where there seems to be one. Sometimes it throws in a load of fish. The mythological analogy is a system of metaphor. It enriches the vision without resorting to montage. . . . I'm not talented as a conceptual thinker but I am in the uses of metaphor" (Stern, 52). I have already discussed Malamud's desire to "enrich" baseball through a metaphorical and symbolic use of myth. What should also be noticed is the way in which the game provides a unifying element within the vast American pattern of diversity. Roy travels from west to east, like the characters in *The Great Gatsby*, an early sign of his quest having the negative overtones of a pilgrimage reversed. However, in accord with the ideals of popular culture, he moves from rural and small town toward urban large city (Chicago and New York); he is the young man fleeing the countryside for the promise of the big city. In his desire to become a part of the national sport, he epitomizes an American dream; in his desire to achieve total success, he illustrates the American entrepreneurial spirit. His failure is a comment on these American ideals, much as Jay Gatsby's failure is. Gatsby does not fully grasp the reality behind his romantic idealism; Roy never grasps the romantic idealism—the hero he could become—beyond the realities of success in baseball, at base a mundane facet of the American Dream.

Roy never approaches the vision of abstract truth encompassed in classic American literature. Malamud writes that "he was like a hunter stalking a bear, a whale, or maybe the sight of a single fleeing star the way he went after that ball" (*TN*, 169). Robert Ducharme remarks: "Thus Roy is put in the tradition of American questers: Daniel Boone or even Ike McCaslin stalking a legendary bear, Captain Ahab pursuing Moby-Dick" (Ducharme, 11). Both Ike McCaslin and Ahab reject the "settlements" for the wilderness; their quest is not carried on in the city in front of masses of people. They eschew entrepreneurial goals for those of the spirit. The same is true of Huck Finn and the river, and Natty Bumppo and the forest and prairie. The goals of all these characters extend beyond the simple realities that so attract Roy: they move in opposite directions from his. Daniel Boone is not, of course, a part of American literature but has spanned the gap between history and legend. Boone's legend is not one that attracts Roy; Roy moves toward the east and the city. Boone is like Ike, Ahab, Huck Finn, and Natty Bumppo: all have fed a part of America's idea of itself; this is not the part, however, to which Roy attaches himself, and while baseball may provide the unifying element mentioned, that unification is of the lowest common denominator. Roy remains a buffoon and does not become a great American hero because bases can be stepping stones to fame but not to grandeur, truth, or freedom.

The language of the novel is suitable for its shifts in tone and plot. Sidney Richman observes that Malamud often uses a "dazzling journalese" and that "throughout the book passages of idiomatic, terse, and slangy prose alternate with passages of lyrical intensity, and often as not the two styles are perfectly integrated, even within the given sentence. . . . The diction is as bifurcated as the hero it describes . . ." (Richman, 44, 46). An instance of this peculiar style can be seen in a description of Roy's first time at bat in a game for the Knights: "He couldn't tell the color of the pitch that came at him. All he could think of was that he was sick to death of waiting, and tongue-out thirsty to begin. The ball was now a dew drop staring him in the eye so he stepped back and swung from the toes" (*TN*, 82). The dual nature of this style parallels the dichotomy of the themes: the mundane aspects of baseball and those of legend and myth; the world of reality and that of fantasy. Roy's vernacular ("sick to death," "tongue-out thirsty") roots the scene in reality; the lyricism ("the color of the pitch," "the ball was now a dew drop") raises it to levels that Malamud explores in his allegorical scenes of legendary heroes and myths. The description is, of course, of Roy's thoughts. But this is not interior monologue or stream-of-consciousness; the author retains his hold on the narrative, his authority as a third-person omniscient narrator. As noted, these shifts can be quite jarring to any sense of consistency, of decorum, in the novel. Because it is often the myth rather than the action of the tale that determines how a character should act, the plot frequently becomes untenable. The shifts in language reflect this problem.

Sidney Richman has called *The Natural* "one of the most baffling novels of the 1950's . . ." (Richman, 28), reflecting remarks by both Granville Hicks and Alfred Kazin. In Malamud's attempt to combine reality and myth both suffer, the human qualities of the characters being undercut by their mythological functions. A train porter introduces dialogue not to be heard on any normal train, raising the question as to whether Eddie is a real porter or merely a minor functionary of the myths that pervade the novel, with his references to lances, wild animals, and obeisance to a hero?

Roy sees nature in symbolic and metaphoric terms: ". . . tormented trees fronting the snaky lake they were passing, trees bent and clawing, plucked white by icy blasts from the black water, their bony branches twisting in many a broken direction" (*TN*, 33). Like the characters, the settings frequently lose their solidity, their reality, through the stress upon symbol and metaphor: a forest or baseball field becoming more—and in terms of reality less—than they actually are.

Malamud's second novel, *The Assistant*, shows some of this orientation toward unreality but is much more coherent in its approach, the unreal elements being reserved for certain aspects of the setting and a few minor characters who nevertheless manage to retain their human solidity. It is not social realism but more of a parable. It shows a great increase in skill from *The Natural*, and remains Malamud's best novel.

Chapter Three
The Assistant

The Nature of Jewishness

Although it is only Malamud's second novel, *The Assistant* moves far beyond *The Natural* in skillfulness and, unlike the earlier novel, contains a strong Jewish theme. Throughout the tale, he uses the image of the Jew and the ethics of Judaism as a standard of behavior. As we have seen, however, his approach to Jewishness is not a parochial one, in that he casts it as a type of secular humanism, a moral code that all good people try to follow. The main characters, Frank Alpine and Morris Bober, carry the weight of the novel. Frank is shown to be imbibing "Jewish" values from Morris and with Morris's death, Frank replaces him both in the store and in terms of having become an ethical man. At the end of the novel, Frank has himself circumcised and becomes a Jew, although in the metaphorical manner in which Malamud uses the term, Frank had already become one.

Morris's definition of Judaism is extremely broad. He tells Frank, "What I worry is to follow the Jewish Law. . . . This means to do what is right, to be honest, to be good. This means to other people. Our life is hard enough. Why should we hurt somebody else?"[1] Frank's rejoinder is telling: "I think other religions have those ideas too . . ." (*TA*, 115).

The point is that although Morris may define Jewish law as the Torah, the basic principles that he chooses to live by are universal. Most of the laws of the Torah are universal, but there are many which Morris chooses to ignore that are directed particularly to the children of Israel. By thus removing any stress on the particular in order to highlight the universal, Morris eliminates the specialness of the Jewish people in world history and dilutes their specific contribution to human ethics.

Universality is stressed again at Morris's funeral, where the rabbi's eulogy proclaims Morris's altruism and downplays the importance of Jewish tradition and adherence to specific Jewish laws, such as synagogue attendance and keeping the dietary requirements. The rabbi must include something about Morris's dilatory adherence to the formal aspects of Judaism, but this lack of specific Jewish practices is really not worth considering. Those aspects of Morris's life that apply to all people are presented as being most important.

Allen Guttmann observes that this definition "turns out to be remarkably like Immanuel Kant's categorical imperative: to want for others what you want for yourself. . . . What Malamud has done is widen the definition of 'Jew' to the point of meaninglessness."[2] Morris is saintly in a human rather than a strictly Jewish sense: "Morris's Jewish Law is synonomous with Malamud's secular moral cole. . . . Becoming a Jew always refers to a secular, personal, inner struggle. . . ."[3] It is this inner struggle of which Morris teaches Frank the value, Morris himself not seeming to be able to live in any other way.

Morris's Jewishness is starkly contrasted with the values of modern America. Indeed, those values are seen as diametrically opposed to the Jewish-humanistic-traditional values for which Morris stands. Honesty and integrity do not lead to success in America, where the possession of money confers a status beyond material wealth. Thus Julius Karp, Morris's successful liquor store–owning neighbor (one of Saul Bellow's "reality instructors") feels no compunction in lecturing Morris about worldly things.

Morris says that when Karp's luck changed and prosperity came his way, "he became wise without brains" (TA, 19). Interestingly, though, despite Karp's seeing Morris as inept and unfortunate, there is something about Morris that Karp admires: "For some reason that was not clear to him Karp liked Morris to like him . . ." (TA, 138). Karp recognizes the moral force behind the failure; Morris is quite possibly the only truly moral man he knows. In his down-at-heel neighborhood, Morris is probably the only man who gives credit to the poor around him, even though many take advantage of his kindness.

Karp breaks his promise and rents a store across the street not to a tailor or shoemaker, but to another grocer. To justify himself he asks Morris, "Who will pay my taxes?" (TA, 15). While Karp is a bit ashamed, it has not stood in the way of business. Even Morris's former partner, Charlie Sobeloff, who cheated Morris out of his share of their business, can tell him he is a dollar short after Morris's first day working for him: the dishonest accusing the honest. Ruth Mandel remarks that "a moral man is an ironic hero simply because he does live by the Law" (Mandel, 262).

The "Law" in America has different meanings. To Nat Pearl the law (not capitalized) offers a way to raise his social class and make money; to

Morris, the Law (always capitalized) has to do with morality and ethical conduct.[4]

A central irony in *The Assistant* lies in the fact that Morris considers himself a failure; that is, he accepts the judgment of Julius Karp, who represents the American ethic that monetary and business success are all that matter, even though Karp himself may be aware of Morris's deeper qualities. The irony moves into paradox when we realize that "Morris' failure is his success" (Cohen, 42). It is because of his inability to succeed in the American business world that Morris is a moral and ethical success. He understands enough to detest Karp's values but wishes that America were the sort of place where morality could lead to practical success. Just before his death, Morris thinks—with Malamud ironically agreeing—"I gave away my life for nothing. It was the thunderous truth" (*TA*, 205). He is buried "in an enormous cemetery—it went on for miles—in Queens" (*TA*, 205). Malamud seems to obliterate Morris; even Ida and Helen think that although he was good, he was a failure: "He made himself a victim. He could, with a little more courage, have been more than he was" (*TA*, 208).

What is Malamud saying here? The novel is a strong condemnation of American values, in that the good and decent people are not honored by society. Not only are they not honored, but society also rewards those who ignore selflessness in favor of selfishness. Malamud's negation of society's values is insidious; in the end, even those who are close to the moral man and who recognize his inherent worth see him as a failure because he must lead a lesser life in material terms. People are unwilling to permit their better selves to come to the fore for fear of the poverty that will result. In such a society, morality is not seen as being worthwhile. American society does not change because of Morris's example, nor does Malamud expect it to. The moral individual must do what is right regardless of its effect or lack of effect. If society considers morality to be synonomous with immaturity, so be it.

Right action is worthwhile as an end in itself, and for its effect on a limited number of individuals. In *The Assistant*, it is Frank Alpine who most benefits from Morris's example and who carries the metaphoric idea of Jewishness to new areas beyond Morris's definition. Even more than Morris, Frank is the primary protagonist of the novel, hence the title. His attitude toward Jews and Jewishness is a negative one for much of the novel until he realizes that, given his dual nature, one that is attracted both to crime and to the spiritual, he must choose the sacrifice and self-discipline that he sees in Morris and assumes to be due to his Jewishness.

There are early hints of Frank's potential. Just after the robbery, he is described as "not bad looking, except for a nose that had been broken and badly set, unbalancing his face" (*TA*, 30). His unbalanced face—his incomplete, unsatisfied self—is caused by a badly set nose. This reference to a Jewish identifying mark is clarified halfway through the book, when Helen begins to see Frank as a possible partner, as gentle and wise: "His crooked nose fitted his face and his face fitted him. It stayed on straight" (*TA*, 120). As Frank apparently becomes responsible and decent (his rape of Helen is still to come), his face ceases to look imbalanced. Indeed, he has changed at this point; the later rape is presented as a starved attempt to achieve a response to his love. At this stage in the story, Helen tries to convince herself that it does not matter that Frank is not Jewish—that love is what is important. Her seeing his crooked nose as fitting and straight implies the broader definition of Jewishness that her father and the rabbi use: a Jewish nose can fit and be straight on a gentile who has certain values.

Another foreshadowing of the role that Morris will take on for Frank and of the significance that Jewishness will have for him occurs early in the story when Morris offers Frank coffee and a roll for helping him with the milk cases: "Jesus, this is good bread" (*TA*, 33), Frank says. Despite the fact that Frank still places great value on the American dream of wealth, there is a side of him that is deeply attracted to goodness and the nonmaterial world of the spirit. Morris may be his Jesus at this point, a giver of bread and a Christlike figure who suffers for others, and he will become a living St. Francis of Assisi to Frank, someone who will teach him how to reject the moneyed values of America for those of an older culture that stresses love and responsibility for others.

As noted earlier, this older culture is not strictly Jewish. "As he accepts faith, he paradoxically eradicates the barriers between theologies."[5] Although Frank is not an observant Roman Catholic, as Morris is not an observant Jew, he interprets Morris's virtue, his sheer ability to endure suffering and yet remain moral, in terms of the Catholic tradition within which he was raised. That Morris detests St. Francis–like poverty is beside the point; it is how he lives under it and the things he is not willing to do to escape it, that make him a saintly figure. Frank thinks that Morris's Jewish tradition must be at the root of his actions, but Malamud makes it clear that any humanistically oriented philosophy can have the same effect. "For Malamud, religion's function is to convey the essentials of the 'good heart'; he has little sympathy either for the ghetto-minded Jew or the parochial Christian."[6]

St. Francis and his life represent an unreachable ideal to Frank, as he sees him as having been "born good." Morris, on the other hand, is flesh and blood; if Morris can come close to the ideal, perhaps Frank can emulate him? In essence, "Morris' saintliness stems from the same sources as Frankie Alpine's worship of St. Francis. . . . Throughout the novel, the young Italian's conversion to Judaism is indistinguishable from his conversion to the saint of Catholicism" (Richman, 71). In both instances, Frank's conversion is to human responsibility and selflessness; both show a rejection of the values of the American Dream.

Helen Bober is a complicating factor in Frank's understanding of Jewishness. She wants the success promised by the American Dream and attempts to achieve it both through reading "great books" and by trying to ensnare Nat Pearl, who is well on his way to material and social success. This side of Helen's character helps us understand why she does not appreciate her father's saintliness.

However, Malamud does present another side to Helen. Her desire for financial and social success does not prevent her from being critical of Nat and ultimately rejecting him and what he stands for. She is also capable of judging Frank favorably in moral terms, although she still hopes to be able to encourage him to go to college and to achieve material success for her. Her problem is that she does not wish to relinquish anything: "Because she desires simultaneously the American Dream and 'something more,' she loses both" (Cohen, 46–47).

To Helen, Jewishness is the religion of her parents, a burden she must consider when deciding whether or not to allow her feelings to flow toward Frank. She never sees it in the metaphoric sense that Morris and Frank do, and she never explains her father's goodness in "Jewish" terms—in terms of the effects of ancient tradition on his understanding of the plight of humanity. Helen rates love and happiness very highly and, ironically, begins to believe that the things that people have in common are more important than those that separate them; that is, she arrives at a judgment of the oneness of humanity through stressing her own individual needs and by eliminating the Torah, whereas her father arrived at this same conclusion through selflessness and an adherance to his particular understanding of the Torah, or the Law.

Ida Bober, Helen's mother, takes a very narrow view of Jewishness; Helen's more broadly "human" definition of individual worth is not convincing to her. Ida reflects the fearful approach to the new world of one who has never been able to become a part of it. Her view of America consists of the little she knows (Jews like Julius and Louis Karp and Sam and Nat Pearl) and the vast amount she does not know and of which she is afraid (Frank and the various non-Jewish customers who occasionally enter the store). She wants Helen to breach the walls of the hostile American fortress, which she was too timid either to conquer herself or to allow Morris to take the necessary risks to succeed in. Her fear has made her a confirmed materialist, and she has taken on the corrupt values of the American world. Thus, she is willing to deceive the prospective buyer Podolsky, and she pushes Helen toward Nat as much for his prospects as for his Jewishness. In the guise of wanting the best for her daughter, Ida denigrates Morris's morality and constantly tries to persuade him to abandon it. Morris wants a better life for Helen, too, but is not willing to abandon his ethics to achieve it, even in the unlikely event that this would work for him. Morris's view of Jewishness as love and responsibility for all humanity is alien to Ida.

In the end it is Frank, Morris's acolyte and substitute son, who will replace his teacher in the store and minister to the needs of the Bober family and the neighborhood. By formally becoming a Jew at the end of the novel, Frank illustrates Malamud's point that "paradoxically, a character may become more Christlike as he becomes more Jewish" (Helterman 1985, 2). Jewish or Christian, it is the heart that counts.

Imprisonment, Suffering, and Redemption

In the course of an interview for the *Paris Review,* the following exchange took place:

> INTERVIEWER: Some critics have commented on this prison motif in your work.
>
> MALAMUD: Perhaps I use it as a metaphor for the dilemma of all men: necessity, whose bars we look through and try not to see. Social injustice, apathy, ignorance. The personal prison of entrapment in past experience, guilt, obsession—the somewhat blind or blinded self, in other words. A man has to construct, invent, his freedom. Imagination helps. A truly great man or woman extends it for others in the process of creating his/her own. (Stern, 54)

To Malamud the exercise of free will is possible but problematic. All human beings are subject to the pressures of circumstance: the inevitable, inescapable aspects of existence. We may try to deny the presence of these "bars," but only by recognizing them have we any chance of acting effectively. Some limitations are external; others are within ourselves, the baggage we carry from our past that prevents effective action in the present. Thus, to speak of human freedom is somewhat foolhardy. However, the struggle to overcome necessity and the limitations of the self is, as Malamud himself has stated, central to his view of the role of humanity. This struggle can clearly be seen in a number of the characters in *The Assistant*.

At the beginning of the novel we are told in Malamud's third-person narration, which also provides overtones of a character's thoughts, "In a store you were entombed" (*TA,* 9). Helen notes that the "living" room is barely used, and Morris concludes that "I slaved my whole life for nothing . . ." (*TA,* 26). The store becomes not only a testing ground for Morris's ability to retain his moral behavior but also a training ground for Frank. Morris tells Frank "a store is a prison" (*TA,* 34), but rather than fleeing, Frank remains. Frank comes to realize that imprisonment is necessary if he is to achieve his moral and spiritual possibilities, particularly if he is to attempt to emulate his hero St. Francis.

The store is Frank's monastery, and his tiny Spartan room, a cell. "As Frank begins to take on the virtues of Bober, the cell becomes a place of monastic illumination. Each act of suffering for Bober and the rest of mankind strips away Frank's worldliness . . ." (Helterman 1985, 50). Thus physical imprisonment is essential for Frank if he is, paradoxically, to release himself from the imprisoning forces within him. What Frank requires is the very imprisonment against which Morris rails: a set of four walls that through self-discipline Frank refuses to leave. To achieve this discipline, he must accept the fact that he is imprisoned more by his own character flaws than by external walls. As Tony Tanner puts it, one sees in Malamud's writing the ways in which "an imprisoned man can forge a new self in his reaction to the imprisoning forces."[7]

Forging a new self leads directly to a great deal of suffering, and it is through suffering that Malamud believes human beings may develop morally. Like the ascetic monk St. Francis, Frank must cease being concerned with material wealth or physical comfort. He must suppress his passions and physical desires and substitute for them an outgoing love for the poor, for humanity as a whole. From Morris, Frank learns to link suffering and love: "Morris's feeding by giving credit to the poor becomes a metaphor for taking care of mankind, and his little neighborhood seems to be a community of nations with its Swedes, Norwegians,

Poles, Germans, Italians, Irish, and Jews" (Helterman 1985, 51). When, toward the end of the novel and literally at Morris's death, Frank becomes Morris both in the sense of replacing him in the store and in taking on his mantle of morality, it is a sign that he has become a new person. The man who climbs out of the grocer's grave only looks like Frank Alpine; he is really Morris reborn, a new Morris who will complete his mentor's life: "Frank will see to Helen's education, one purpose of which is to give posthumous meaning to the grocer's pathetic life. Thus each life gains meaning by what it gives to the next, and the divine circle of the Law, of doing for others, curves back on the point of its origin: the meaning of Morris Bober's life."[8]

One problem with Malamud's stress on the value of suffering is that it may be seen as masochistic, thus reducing its moral value. Sidney Richman states that "though they would never admit it and cannot understand it, both Morris and Frank like the store. Such refinement of masochism—and there is no other word for it—is in many ways unprecedented in American literature" (Richman, 50–51). Is Frank's self-punishment really necessary for him to become a moral man? Does Morris have to be a *schlimazel* to be a saint? While accepting that Morris's ethic permits Frank to place "his suffering in a moral system that gives it value," Robert Ducharme questions "the ultimate effect of a value system that sanctifies the acceptance of suffering, that exhalts victimhood, and makes failure into success" (Ducharme, 63). However admirable Frank's efforts at self-improvement, at forcing out the bad and bringing forth the good in himself, there is a point at which the price he must pay seems too high.

Malamud's basic idea is the same as that of the great Russian novelist Fyodor Dostoyevski: through suffering one can achieve redemption. For Dostoyevski, however, the suffering is not as clearly chosen as is Frank's, although both authors stress the importance of suffering borne on account of love, this being a most important element if salvation is to be at all possible. It is possible, as Sheldon Grebstein points out, to find the source of Malamud's ethic in the Bible: "Malamud thus follows in the ancient Jewish tradition of the prophets, Amos, Jeremiah, the Second Isaiah, who announce suffering to be the Jew's special destiny, evidence of his unique covenant with God, proof of God's concern in that only those who are loved are chastised, and the means of the Jew's peculiar awareness of his identity. . . ."[9]

If the suffering depicted in *The Assistant* is viewed as masochism, it becomes difficult to see it as a means of developing insight into the value of love and selflessness. It becomes even more difficult to see it leading to a type of salvation or redemption. The biblical interpretation places this suffering in a much wider context: that of Judaism, the Jewish people, and Jewish history. In this sense, suffering may provide a meaning of life, placing the Jew in the context of the divine—or the divinely chosen. However, this does not answer Ducharme's criticism of a system that "sanctifies the acceptance of suffering" and "exhalts victimhood." Rather than acceptance, the attitude presented in the novel can be seen instead as one of understanding, as Morris tells Frank, "If you live, you suffer. Some people suffer more, but not because they want" (*TA,* 116).

Morris does not seek out or enjoy suffering; he simply recognizes the human condition for what it is. Jews may suffer more than some others because they are Jews (the theme of the Jews' place in history being one that Malamud will explore at length in *The Fixer*). Morris understands, however, that Jews do not possess a monopoly on suffering: it is a part of existence for everyone. The important thing is to take this unfortunate, unavoidable condition of life and turn it into something positive, something of worth to humanity. So, Morris adds, "I suffer for you. . . . I mean you suffer for me" (*TA,* 116); that is, we are all in the same situation and must have sympathy and compassion for each other.

It is noteworthy that "Morris is the English equivalent for Moses . . ." (Freedman, 162). Moses led the Israelites through 40 years of suffering in the wilderness until they, without him, were able to enter the promised land. While the nature of the "promised land" in *The Assistant* is highly problematic, Frank is certainly better off morally, and possibly physically, at the end of the novel. Morris, Frank's Job-like teacher and guide, takes his son/assistant far enough along the path to righteousness that he can carry on unaided, his own formerly submerged strength of character in control of his less admirable qualities.

The name Morris Bober is very similar to that of Martin Buber, probably the foremost Jewish philosopher of the twentieth century. Malamud wrote to the critic Peter Hays that "he had only a very general acquaintance with Buber's work when he wrote *The Assistant* and did not intend to identify Morris Bober with the renowned philosopher."[10] Despite Malamud's comment, it is remarkable how closely the ideas and development of the characters in the novel parallel the philosophy set forth in Buber's famous work, *I and Thou*.

In the 1970 translation of Buber's book, Walter Kaufmann stresses *You* rather than *Thou* as a more accurate rendering of Buber's German word *Du*. *Thou* he says is too formal, given Buber's stress upon human relationships.[11] In the context of *The Assistant*, Frank must move from the "I-It" stance that he takes at the beginning of the novel to an "I-You" one. Buber writes: "The basic word I-You can only be spoken with one's whole being. The basic word I-It can never be spoken with one's whole being."[12] When we first meet him, Frank sees Morris as just a Jew and later sees Helen only in terms of lust. He is not that far removed from Ward Minogue, his partner in robbing Morris. However, there are signs that Frank may have the capability to move to I-You relationships, in that he helps Morris and idolizes St. Francis. Thus, there is hope that in time his "whole being" can be engaged.

Buber writes: "Love is responsibility of an I for a You . . ." (Buber, 66); "Man becomes an I through a You" (Buber, 80); "Persons appear by entering into relation to other persons" (Buber, 112). The essential quality that Morris possesses is his ability to view and treat others, including those he does not particularly like, not in terms of abstractions or neutrals—"Its"—but as human beings—"Yous." Through Morris's influence, Frank is able to defeat the negative aspects of his nature and bring the positive ones to the forefront, but until he is able to establish true relationships with others, he cannot be a good man. Once he can see others as "Yous," he not only achieves human goodness, but he also can approach an understanding of the eternal. In terms of Judaism, man must make the everyday sacred and see the Godhead in his everyday human relations. Buber states that "the relation to a human being is the proper metaphor for the relation to God—as genuine address is here accorded a genuine answer" (Buber, 151). Morris not only relates to people but to God. Through his changed view of others, Frank, too, eventually achieves this relationship.

Helen's role in Frank's redemption, in his becoming a moral individual through responsibility and selflessness and, concomitantly, his achieving a sense of God, is not as important as Morris's, but she has importance nevertheless. Malamud's depiction of their relationship also can be seen in terms of Buber's philosophy: "When a man loves a woman so that her life is present in his own, the You of her eyes allows him to gaze into a ray of the eternal You. But if a man lusts after the 'ever repeated triumph'—you want to dangle before his lust a phantom of the eternal?" (Buber, 154). From climbing up the air shaft to look at Helen naked in the bathroom, Frank moves toward a feeling of love for her. He does rape her, however, and one may question Malamud's treatment of this as a sign of Frank's starved love and a result of Helen's having wrongly rejected him: "A Malamudian irony: Helen is able to love Frank only until he makes love to her; the fact debauches the illusion" (Baumbach 1963, 454). However, unlike Frank, Helen is depicted as a character who does not really grow in understanding. Frank wonders whether she has learned anything from the great literature she has read. She uses the books as a means of self-improvement but gains no real insight into her life until she is attracted, despite misgivings, by Frank's moral growth, which elicits a response from the better side of her own nature, giving Frank someone for whom to sacrifice.

The rape marks a turning point for Frank after which all the previous events coalesce in a determination finally to take control of his life: "The wrong he had done her was never out of his mind. He hadn't intended wrong but he had done it; now he intended right" (*TA,* 168). Love replaces lust, and seeing the "eternal You" becomes a possibility.

Living for love makes Frank into an assistant for the third time: ". . . first to Ward Minogue, then to Morris, and finally to Helen and her mother . . . (Hays, 230). Although neither Helen nor Ida are particularly worthy of Frank's great sacrifice, that is not the main point. They provide a focus for his moral change, and it is that change that is at the heart of the novel. Moreover, it is the ability to see as "You" those people who are not saintly that shows real moral growth. The suffering that Frank takes willingly upon himself leads directly to whatever redemption Malamud allows. He is plunged to the lowest depths of himself (robbery, rape) before elevation is possible, testing "his actual self against his ideal of himself" (Baumbach 1963, 455).

The question arises as to the price Malamud exacts for Frank's redemption. Philip Roth thinks that the price is too high and the method by which this redemption is achieved unjust: "But oh how punitive is this redemption! We might almost take what happens to the bad goy when he falls into the hands of the good Jews as an act of enraged Old Testament retribution visited upon him by the wrathful Jewish author—if it weren't for the moral pathos and gentle religious coloration. . . ."[13] Like Yasha Mazur at the close of Isaac Bashevis Singer's novel *The Magician of Lublin,* Frank has chosen entombment as being necessary for his redemption; he is as much a prisoner in the store, slaving his life away for Ida and Helen, as Yasha is in his cell. Also, he has himself circumcised, an act of self-punishment to atone for Helen's rape as well as a ritual required for male converts to Judaism. We read that "The pain enraged and inspired him" (*TA,* 222); Roth stresses the pain, Malamud the inspiration. The inspiration derives from Frank's hard-won ability to discipline his baser instincts, and we have seen how difficult it has been for him to keep them in check. Similarly in *The Magician of Lublin,* Yasha tells us that the means necessary to control the passions depend on their strength. Thus, rather than viewing the situation as Malamud's Jewish revenge upon non-Jews for, perhaps, the vicissitudes of Jewish history, it would be more useful to examine closely the history of failure that Frank relates throughout the novel. He sees, quite accurately, that the store, "Jewishness," and the Bobers are his last chance. The alternative for him is the road taken by Ward Minogue. It must also be recalled that Frank's monastic choice is not particularly Jewish, as indeed Yasha Mazur's hermitlike existence is not. Frank chooses within his own Catholic tradition, and it is not by accident that St. Francis, a paradigm of poverty and suffering for the sake of the soul, is his hero.

At the end of the novel Frank does not become an object of pilgrimage, as Yasha does. However, there are signs that he may develop into the moral center of the neighborhood, much as Morris was. He treats the local poor with compassion and, to pass the time in the virtually empty store, reads the Bible and thinks "there are parts of it he could have written himself" (*TA,* 222). We are left with the image of a man sitting alone in a cell-like store, reading the Bible, and thinking of St. Francis. His redemption is complete.

Form and Content

When Malamud was asked about the source of *The Assistant,* he answered: "Mostly my father's life as a grocer, though not necessarily my father. Plus three short stories, sort of annealed in a single narrative: 'The Cost of Living' and 'The First Seven Years'—both in *The Magic Barrel.* And a story I wrote in the forties, 'The Place Is Different Now . . .'" (Stern, 53). In addition to these, there are seven tales that foreshadow *The Assistant* (see chapter 10). The stories contain themes that are developed much more thoroughly in The Assistant: poverty as both moral teacher and grinding adversary; insights into the human heart occurring in the most unlikely settings; the importance of moral responsibility and human goodness over materialism; and the ever-present pressure of the past, with its mistakes, unavoidable disasters, and unfulfilled dreams.

Although *The Assistant* has overtones of naturalism, Malamud does not adhere to a strict determinism. The characters do possess some free will, although looking at Morris one may wonder how much. However,

Morris could have chosen to become a pharmacist; we see Helen making a number of choices regarding the men in her life; and Frank decides to change what appears to be an immutable life pattern. Nor is the ending pessimistic in terms of what Frank has achieved, moving as he has from the world of Ward Minogue to one of caring for humanity.

The novel is only partly realistic. Tony Tanner observes that "although the plight of the Bober family is real enough, the novel moves effortlessly towards fable. . . ."[14] The actual location of the store is never stated; it exists in a poverty-striken area that has the feel of permanence and timelessness, and its actual location is irrelevant. What is stressed is the metaphoric and symbolic nature of the action, with the setting—the neighborhood and the store—providing an enclosed world of material deprivation wherein the characters either work through their spiritual odysseys or fail to recognize the central importance of the spiritual and are left, in Malamud's terms, failures.

Moving through this mythic wasteland setting are minor characters who exhibit both realistic and fantastic aspects. The "Polisheh" is a reminder of the very real anti-Semitic world of Eastern Europe that Morris fled. Al Marcus, dying of cancer, uncomplainingly fights death and makes the most of what life has dealt him. Breitbart, also accepting the suffering that life has meted out to him, trudges through the neighborhood selling "lights," a symbol of hope. The "Macher" is a highly symbolic figure, diabolic with his red beard and relation to fire. All four characters lean, in varying degrees, toward unreality but remain also part of the real world.

Irony is the basic stance taken throughout the novel, ironic affirmation being seen by a number of critics as central to Malamud's approach. The striving of the characters to achieve their goals is usually undercut by an opposite character trait that prevents their success or by a result that is far different than that which was desired. Morris's goodness achieves neither material rewards nor respect from his family. While Malamud admires Morris, he is ruthless in not permitting him any satisfaction or fulfillment as a result of his goodness. As mentioned earlier, even Morris's burial seems to annihilate his memory as it takes place in a huge, anonymous cemetery. Affirmation occurs only through a sense that goodness is worthwhile as an end in itself and through Frank's transformation on account of Morris's example.

Through Frank's analysis of his life he even recognizes the irony in his own character. Virtually everything he has done has had negative results, largely because of an inherent character flaw. Despite this, his hero is St.

Francis and he longs to be and do good. When he finally achieves his goal, the result is not physical freedom but a form of imprisonment. For Frank, physical imprisonment in the store is equal to spiritual freedom, an irony that he must accept if he is to remain moral. However, his victory looks remarkably like a defeat.

Ihab Hassan has written that "the achievement of Malamud's style, which survives his ironic play, lies in the author's capacity to convey both hope and agony in the rhythms of Yiddish speech."[15] The Yiddish-English dialect that Malamud uses, most effectively with Morris and Ida, shows some of his characters to be a part of two cultures and, in many ways, attached to neither. The Bobers do not live in a Jewish neighborhood, but they are not part of the wider non-Jewish American world. Ida's English, heavily inflected with Yiddishisms, aids in stereotyping her as a narrow, fearful, nagging, immigrant Jewish woman. She always fears the worst, and she has reason to. She lives in poverty and feels that she has no control over her life, particularly since Morris persuaded her to leave their former, Jewish neighborhood for their present one. Indeed, everything she is afraid will happen does. A typical exchange follows:

> "The Italyener," he said, drying himself, "bought this morning across the street."
>
> She was irritated. "Give him for twenty-nine dollars five rooms so he should spit in your face."
>
> "A cold-water flat," he reminded her.
>
> "You put in gas radiators."
>
> "Who says he spits? This I didn't say."
>
> "You said something to him not nice?" (*TA*, 10)

Much of the novel's language does not have this quick give and take but is rather flat, reflecting the passage of endless, deadened days for all the Bobers. There is nothing to look forward to for any of them. Understatement is commonly used to describe events and to create a tone of flat, dull repetitiveness. In the dialogue just cited, however, Malamud manages to combine the seriousness of the Bober's plight (they cannot even keep their tenant as a customer) with a hint of humor in the squabbling of Morris and Ida. The Yiddish dialect itself, with its occasionally odd diction and inverted sentence structure, adds to this sense of both tragedy and humor because it implies, on the one hand, incomprehension of and ineptitude in dealing with a situation, while on the other hand it contains the comedy inherent in an attempt to understand a situation in broken English.

In fact the novel is not funny, as Ruth Mandel comments: "The whole weight of the novel crushes laughter. It is unlaughable comedy about the funny little man who is not funny at all. This is the artistic achievement—the grotesque mixture of high seriousness with what seems funny and yet is not. All of which heightens the pathos" (Mandel, 266). Here can be seen overtones of the influence of Charlie Chaplin, to which Malamud attested. Chaplin's famous tramp certainly is funny, much more so than Morris Bober, but there is a strong element of pathos in Chaplin's character that always causes a hitch in the laughter.

Malamud manages to use the very harshness of the situation to create a type of humor that stems directly from the Yiddish tradition. This humor owes its effect to "the wile of Yiddish folklore, the ambiguous irony of the Jewish joke. Pain twisted into humor twists humor back into pain" (Hassan, 200). Through omniscient authorial narration with frequent movements into the minds of the characters, Malamud manages to gain absolute control for himself as author while still providing a sense of immediacy and intimacy. We are drawn directly into Morris's musings on the bitterness of his life, presented through the ironies of Jewish humor: "Years ago Karp had spent much time in the back of the grocery, complaining of his poverty as if it were a new invention and he its first victim" (*TA,* 24).

Ida is too humorless, too immersed in her own despondency to be able to view her situation in ironic terms. Helen can see the irony in her unrealizable goals and does, at times, see the situation as Morris does: "At the end you were sixty and had less than at thirty. It was, she thought, surely a talent . . ." (*TA,* 19).

The characters are differentiated further through their speech. Most of the time Helen's speech patterns and thoughts are presented not in Yiddish dialect but in good standard American English, perhaps better than the average. Her language lacks colloquialisms and slang and is suitable to a somewhat bookish person who desires self-improvement and shows these characteristics in her speech. It is even superior to that of Nat Pearl, the law student, who lapses into profanity at stressful moments, and it differs from Frank's speech, which is markedly colloquial. However, it is noteworthy that Malamud presents Frank's speech as containing far less profanity than Ward Minogue's. Like Helen, Frank is trying to improve himself, and this may be the reason for his being granted a superior level of speech. Through Malamud's subtle shifts from

third-person omniscient narrator to interior monologue, we see that
Frank is capable of lyricism, as when he thinks of Helen's body:
". . . the breasts like small birds in flight, her ass like a flower" (TA,
72). Frank's words and thoughts of St. Francis are always presented
through lyrical language.

The character whose speech is least affected by thematic concerns is
Louis Karp, a simple down-to-earth boy who, like all the other sons in
the novel (Nat, Frank, even Ward), courts Helen's love in one way or
another.[16] His language is uneducated street slang, which reflects his
basically unthinking attitude toward life: "Say, baby, let's drop this deep
philosophy and go trap a hamburger. My stomach complains" (TA, 43).
He is gentler than his father, who, while coming from a similar background to Morris, does not possess his innate goodness. Julius Karp's
language, having Yiddish inflexions but lacking all warmth and wisdom, used to present harsh realities and ignorant of the heart, also reflects
in its spare directness the nature of the speaker.

Malamud's use of language is part of the American literary tradition in
that "it is a significant development and expansion of the American
colloquial style, established as a vital literary medium by Mark Twain.
The Jewish style is for the first time in our literary history a voice that
conveys ethnic characteristics, a special sort of sensibility, and the quality
of a foreign language, yet remains familiar and eloquent to non-Jews"
(Grebstein, 20–21).

In addition to adhering to American literary traditions, Malamud
used universal myths as a basis for the novel's structure. In particular, the
movement of the seasons underscores the events of the plot, with the tale
beginning in early November and ending in April. The narrative covers
two years and in some aspects parallels the use of myth in The Natural.
Here, however, the seasonal symbolism and the theme of man's
fall, death, and redemption support rather than control character development. Malamud has said that "the chief business of the writer is 'the
drama of personality fulfilling itself'" (Richman, 52). In The Assistant,
Malamud placed this drama first and the mythological structure clearly
second.

Winter is setting in just as Frank, having reached the level of petty
criminality, begins the story with a load of failures from his past. He had
started his life in California and has arrived in New York: a movement
from west to east, in American terms a pilgrimage reversed. The Bobers
also have reached a low point. Morris has been imprisoned in the store for
21 years, the age at which an individual attains his majority, his full civil

rights. Morris and his family are without freedom and future, and he is very much aware of this. Morris lives in the dreams of a youth that is long past; Ephraim, his son, died of an ear sickness and so never heard his father's teachings; Helen remains unmarried, so there are no grandchildren; Ida complains about lost opportunities and, also, can see no future.

Frank carries the main burden of movement from a past of failure and criminality (a fall); to slipping into Morris's grave (death); to emerging from the grave, taking on Morris's mantle, and becoming his "son," one who can provide a future for himself and for Morris's ideals (redemption). Like Roy Hobbs in *The Natural,* Frank revitalizes the wasteland; he undergoes the sacred initiation of circumcision in the spring, the time of rebirth. His rebirth, both as Morris and as a Jew, takes the novel through the seasonal cycle, ending at Passover, the festival that celebrates freedom from slavery. Thus, Morris dies and Frank replaces him in the spring of the year; Morris had misjudged the time when spring arrived, but Frank, his young replacement, has read the signs accurately and completed the cycle from death to rebirth that parallels the seasonal changes in the novel.

Helen takes on the role of fertility goddess: "To emphasize this role of hers, Malamud frequently has her described in terms of obvious symbols of fertility: flowers (harbingers of spring's renewal) and birds. . . . The bird and flower symbols, especially the former, are also significant because of Frank's symbolic relationship to St. Francis of Assisi" (Hays, 224). Almost in spite of herself, Helen provides Frank with one of the bases for his redemption. There is at least the implication that, eventually, Frank will marry Helen, fructifying Morris's daughter, the prime fertility symbol in the novel.

Father-son relationships form another underlying structural pattern. There are three biological father-son relationships in the novel; in none has the father succeeded in producing a moral son. Showing no love for his son Ward, Detective Minogue desires only respectability, something Ward never provides. Sam Pearl bets on horses and has produced in Nat only a materialist and social climber. Julius Karp is a complete materialist who accepts that his son Louis steals from him. He believes that money is everything and will even buy Helen. Selling liquor has made him rich, whereas selling food has left Morris in poverty, a reflection of American values. None of these relationships is morally fruitful.

A fourth father-son relationship exists between Morris and Frank. Though not related biologically, they nonetheless provide what each needs for his own fulfillment. Although at first Morris does not fully recognize Frank as a suitable substitute for Ephraim, eventually he is touched by Frank's persistent attempts to change. Morris needs a son, and Frank, an orphan, needs a father who can teach him to value the right things. In the sense that a father guides his son in the right direction, this relationship is a more successful father-son pairing than that of the natural fathers and sons. However, as Robert Ducharme observes: ". . . here, too, there is irony in the displacement pattern, for Frank finds a father in Morris only to replace him through death, and he finds a girl to love in Helen only to assume a selfless, essentially paternal, role toward her as provider for her education" (Ducharme, 38).

As I have noted previously, irony is an essential aspect of *The Assistant* and a device that Malamud uses throughout his work. Irony assumes a complex, unsure world where the obvious may not be the best and where achievement and success may not be what is of most worth. This view of existence can be seen in Malamud's next novel, *A New Life,* as clearly as in *The Assistant.*

Chapter Four

A New Life

Social Criticism in Cascadia

Malamud's third novel is set in a much more identifiable place than is *The Assistant,* reflecting the 12 years he lived in Corvallis, Oregon, and was an instructor in the English Department at Oregon State College. *A New Life* follows both *The Natural* and *The Assistant* in being critical of aspects of American culture. However, whereas the earlier novels stress the limitations of American values in terms of national ideals (heroism, success, the American Dream), *A New Life* focuses more closely upon these values in a particular time (the 1950s) and place (the West). It is the first Malamud novel that engages political issues that concerned America nationally and internationally: "*A New Life* is oddly enough one of the few novels not journalism, of the mid-century, that contains specific speculations on Korea, the cold war, McCarthyism, Hiss and Chambers, loyalty oaths, the plight of liberalism, the definition and the duties of radicalism."[1] These issues are intertwined with a strong sense of the setting: the American West with its mythological overtones. Indeed, the setting provides much of the basis for the social criticism that pervades the novel.

Upon Seymour Levin's arrival in Cascadia, he is struck by the sheer beauty of the environment, something lacking in New York City. For a short time this beauty deludes him into thinking that Cascadia is the ideal place to begin his new life. He also has visions of the pioneers coming through the area in covered wagons and of his being in touch with the real America, a healing place, the "West as redemptive environment . . ." (Alter 1981, 32). This view is influenced by Levin's respect for the ideas of Thoreau and Emerson who, of course, saw in nature signs of the creation that could lead an individual into himself, there to see the divine. Thoreau and Emerson "serve as mentors whose philosophy frequently prevents Levin from an accurate evaluation of his adopted community and contributes to the comic romanticism that makes the New Yorker an American Quixote" (Alter 1981, 32). That is, for a time Levin superimposes upon the natural beauty of Cascadia ideas that relate that beauty to the people who live surrounded by it, as if they gained in stature by their mere presence among the mountains and forests. In due course he does learn that the spirit of the Westerners is not synonomous with the natural beauty of the place.

Levin brings with him from the East all of the myths that America has built into its idea of the West. The West is Eden and paradise, a place for new beginnings. It is also the bastion of democracy and rugged individualism. As the continent was settled in the East, the West served as a "safety valve" for the more adventurous or land hungry, the border between civilization and savagery marking that not only between settled and newcomer but also between those who still looked to Europe for culture and recognition and those who turned their backs on the established codes of both Europe and the East in favor of creating a new, more vibrant society. Such, briefly, are some of the attributes that have been given to the American West. Many of these encomiums are shown to be unwarranted, as Malamud has Levin discover: "He expects the frontier virtues of freedom, independence, courage, and accord with nature. One by one these expectations are shattered" (Helterman 1985, 53), particularly in relation to democracy, which is defined by the community of Cascadia as the freedom to do as everyone else does.

In mythic terms, Levin can be seen as an Adam, one who enters Eden in innocent acceptance of the Western ideal and suffers a fall. Levin's innocence is false, however: he had already fallen in the East. He has gone west to raise himself up but, ironically, must fall (that is, fail) again in order to be redeemed—a very different result from the consequences of his Eastern fall. The parallel between the two situations is that Levin is unable to cope with the demands of either locale; he has carried his disabilities with him to the West. Indeed, the novel harps on his battle to overcome his past (for "past" read personality or character). In the end, Levin cannot escape from his old life by simply fitting into a romantic myth of the West; however, Pauline, his colleague's wife and Levin's future mistress, provides the basis for his being able to accept the love and responsibility that lies within him, so substituting for acceptance of western society and its values more valuable inner qualities. Although it is not what he wanted or expected, Levin does achieve a new life.

His new existence receives an early impetus from the career of Leo Duffy, whose former office Levin inhabits and whom Gerald Gilley, Pauline's husband, calls a "disagreeable radical who made a lot of trouble."[2] Duffy was an outsider in Cascadia, a Roman Catholic from

Chicago, just as Levin is an outsider, a Jew from New York. Leslie Fiedler observes that on the level of fable, *A New Life* "reflects the essential comedy of the West after it has been mythicized by one generation of immigrants and is invaded by the next and the next and the next, being an account of two provincialities meeting head-on in a kind of mutual incomprehension. . . ."[3]

Duffy and Levin are not only aware of the myths of the West but they also have a much tougher set of ideals that involves judging and testing whether the myths actually have any substance. One critic feels that "Duffy is used as a myth—the myth of the liberal radical" (Mandel, 271). There is an element of stereotyping here in the assumption that non-WASP urban Americans in the 1950s were more left-wing, more critical of society, than were rural WASPs, even if the latter were highly educated. While this was true before the Second World War, it is debatable whether it could still be assumed after it, when Italian and Jewish Americans were largely second- and third-generation Americans. It may be more useful to focus on the difficulty of city-bred people in coping with the dramatically different life led in rural America. While both Duffy and Levin certainly have much to criticize in the repressive and un-American attitudes of the Cascadians, both are "tenderfeet" who suffer from culture shock, which partly explains their inability to understand remarks such as Pauline's that "people here are satisfied" (*NL*, 25) and "there are people here, originally from the Plains states or the Midwest, who swear Easchester is paradise" (*NL*, 26).

The orientation of Cascadia College is foreshadowed at the beginning of the novel when Gerald Gilley cannot show Levin the Humanities building, as it is hidden by the Chemical Engineering and "Ag" buildings. Gilley has lost interest in literature, preferring to teach composition. He is working on a picture book of American authors and is an avid photographer of Americana; he has won prizes for his photos of subjects like "Pioneer Farmhouse." Pauline tells Levin that Gilley is "in love with Americana" (*NL*, 23); this will prove notable for its irony when Levin realizes that Gilley's love of American ideals is sadly lacking, his standards relying instead on those of the townspeople. He easily yields to public pressure to remove an anthology from the literature survey course when a millhand, the father of one of the students, objects to a Hemingway story because it contains some sexual scenes.

Levin believes that the liberal arts "teach what the human spirit is or may achieve . . ." (*NL*, 34). He refers to Socrates and to the severe limitations of a purely vocational education, which is what Cascadians want. They are not interested in close examination of self or society. Marcus Klein refers to Cascadia as "a society under an iron discipline of amiability. . . . The imagination, the ideals, the sap have gone out of it" (Klein, 251).

One of the reasons for this state of affairs is the effect of the myths discussed earlier: "They cannot risk admitting to discontent or dissatisfaction, to anguish, despair, or failure. To do so would be to confess the defeat of the paradisal dream, and to reveal the society and their lives as shams" (Alter 1981, 46). What Levin, Duffy, and Pauline see is that human needs and political realities demand more involved and complicated responses than the locals are able to give them.

The political climate of the 1950s heightens the sense of the powerlessness of a liberal in the Far West. As Levin considers the cold war, the Korean War, and Senator McCarthy's House Un-American Activities Committee, the unconfident part of him feels a certain comfort: "America was in the best sense of a bad term, un-American. Levin was content to be hidden amid forests and mountains in an unknown town in the Far West" (NL, 96). Because he is a liberal and has such faith in the value of the liberal arts, this comfort cannot last, even given his fear of failing again and his desire to keep a low profile. The conflict between the realization of his new life and standing up for his principles follows Levin throughout the novel.

Just as America saw itself as God's country, an ideal democratic state, the West viewed itself as the perfection of this ideal. There is, however, a contradiction here: "If Eden signifies that which is faultless, and democracy that which is choice and change, then there may very well be an intrinsic contradiction within American culture, believing that one may inhabit Eden at the same time that one dwells in a democracy" (Alter 1981, 36). The townspeople, college faculty, and students prefer to preserve the illusion of Eden and surrender democracy; the few who disagree with this approach tread carefully and are afraid.

C. D. Fabrikant is the department scholar who teaches a course on liberalism in American literature. After telling Levin something of the glories of Cascadian history, with its explorers, pioneers, and Indian fighters, he says of their descendants: "Their great fear is that tomorrow will be different from today. I've never seen so many pygmies in my life" (NL, 109). Unfortunately Fabrikant, although he tells us that he has been outspoken in the past, shows much restraint in expressing critical views in the department because he wants a promotion.

His enemies are Professor Fairchild and Gerald Gilley, who represent the "pygmies" in the department. Fairchild holds forth in the coffee room on creeping socialism and the horrors of the New Deal; no one questions him, and Levin senses fear. He notes how "Fairchild and Gilley, seemingly equalitarian, autocratically ran things. Climate or moral climate?" (*NL,* 260–261).

Levin realizes that basketball provides the town's big emotional outlet and wishes it also could come from a good book. This is clearly foreign territory to him[4]: "He must learn about Cascadia the same way Frankie Alpine learned the grocery business from Morris" (Cohen, 62). Like Carol Kennicott in *Main Street,* an outsider who tries to reform the town, Levin ought to learn about the people and place before forming his views, although his views on the Cascadians' conservatism in all areas are basically sound, as are Carol's. Like her, though, his methods of trying to change their attitudes may not be correct, given his brief time among them. He should have taken the time to try to understand why they think the way they do.

Levin does have a right to expect more from the faculty of the college than from the townspeople. The president, Dr. Labhart, has said that "Plato, Shelley, and Emerson have done more harm than good to society" (*NL,* 276). His very name implies a heart joined to technology and not the humanities. This practical, nonspiritual orientation exists even in the head of the English Department, Professor Fairchild, who says, "More than one of my former students have returned to tell me that mastering English grammar was the turning point of their lives" (*NL,* 57–58). Like Labhart, his view of human development is that of a technician.

In a scene that is pure black comedy, Levin finds himself to be the only person to hear Fairchild's dying words:

> "The mys—mystery—of the in-fin—in-fin—"
>
> "Infinite."
>
> "In-fin-i-tive. Have you con-sidered its possi-bil-i-ties? (*NL,* 292)

Malamud's criticism of Fairfield is scathing. He is buried "not too far from the graves of the pioneers . . ." (*NL,* 292), another telling criticism, given Fairchild's lack of pioneer stature—his safe, restrictive, unimaginative worldview. This is what, as Fabrikant has said, the new Cascadians have become.

Levin decides to risk his future by running for the chairmanship of the department. He feels that liberal principles must be supported regardless of the cost. There is certainly a hint of conceit and foolishness in this action since Levin is not presented as totally worthy of support, in part because of what Gilley and Fabrikant try to explain as the practical difficulties of making all of the changes at once. There is also the problem of his affair with Gilley's wife. Nonetheless, Levin is more principled than the rest, despite having more to lose than either Gilley or Fabrikant. When he tells his students, while Bullock, a conservative English professor, eavesdrops at his door, that the liberal arts "teach what's for sale in a commercial society, and what had better not be. That democracy is a moral philosophy and can't be defended by lopping off its head" (*NL*, 265), he is surely stating the truth.

In the end he fails, inevitably, to transform Cascadia. But Malamud makes it clear that one flawed man can have an effect. *The Elements* will be replaced after 30 years on the syllabus; a Great Books program will be instituted; and Fabrikant is growing a beard, perhaps a sign that he will become a more committed reformer. We now must turn to Levin's personal development, which, while being related to his social criticism, becomes at times a separate plot strand, one of the structural flaws of the novel.

Growth and Development

Levin's development begins before his arrival in Cascadia, in his attempt to extricate himself from the legacy of his thieving father and suicide mother. He has lifted himself out of a filthy cellar where he lay in a drunken stupor, having had a vision of the beauty of life. He says that "I then became a man of principle" (*NL*, 196). He comments frequently on the ways in which the past intrudes into the present, one of his "insights" being, "The new life hangs on an old soul . . ." (*NL*, 61). Ruth Mandel remarks that Levin "does not spend most of his time struggling with an ugly past and bad habits in a way comparable to Frank Alpine's real conflicts. . . . After all is said and done he is more the victim of circumstance and the actions of other people than a vigorous, active character" (Mandel, 271). I think that Mandel underestimates the influence of the past upon Levin. He rarely has an experience in nature, at the college, or with people that does not lead him to dredge up from his past some incident or feeling that affects his present state of mind or a decision he is making. Like Frank, he has to cope with the present and with old habits and fears of failure, old mistakes and a tendency to doubt the possibility of success. For both characters, present possibilities can only be seen in terms of success in overcoming past limitations.

Levin says early in the novel: "The times are bad but I've decided I'll have no other" (*NL,* 24). That is, for him the times have always been bad, McCarthy and the cold war notwithstanding. He must make of them whatever can be made. He must try not to let the past destroy his present; this is one of the reasons he remembers it, quoting Santayana to Gilley: ". . . if you don't remember the past you were condemned to relive it" (*NL,* 280). Levin is more than "the victim of circumstance," as he chooses courses of action that, because of the influence of his past, he finds he must choose.

Levin grows through love, and it is his growing ability to love rather than his having come to the West that provides the basis for his new life. As he discovers with his student Nadalee, he is not one for casual affairs: sex has to lead to love and possibly to marriage for him to be able to continue a relationship. His affair with Pauline begins through loneliness but develops in Malamud's comic fashion into love and beyond it. Levin realizes that he must make a commitment when he suffers a "pain in the butt" after every instance of sexual intercourse with her. He realizes that his suffering has been caused by "withholding what he had to give. He then gave birth. Love ungiven had caused Levin's pain" (*NL,* 208).

Fear of the past, with its sufferings, had prevented him from committing himself wholeheartedly to Pauline. Although he needs it, he is afraid of love, afraid of losing control of his emotions, so trying to repress them. He feels that it is only through self-discipline that he can create his new life, and love is not what he had planned, because where it might lead is unpredictable. He is attracted by the idea of love but not necessarily by the particular person or the reality of it. There is also the burden of Pauline's present and past: her husband, children, and neuroses. Does Levin really want to cope with these?

Like Helen for Frank Alpine in *The Assistant,* Pauline may not be a particularly selfless or admirable person with whom Levin should fall in love. However, for Malamud, it is not the person eliciting the feeling of love that is of paramount importance but the love that is elicited: "We realize that it is not so much these particular women that Malamud is interested in presenting as worthy of so much sacrifice. Yet they represent possible objects for the love that Frank and Levin come to believe in—an unselfish love . . ." (Mandel, 264). Levin gives in to his feelings and accepts his love for Pauline. This leads him toward a new life, but a different one than he had thought was possible; eventually, he says, "Love is life" (*NL,* 238), thus showing the change in understanding that has taken place in him.

For Levin, and for Malamud, love is never uncomplicated. While it is an essential part of a protagonist's development toward a secular redemption (something that Roy Hobbs never completely achieves and that Frank Alpine does), Malamud qualifies love in that it does not necessarily fulfill all of a character's needs. It is inextricably entwined with a sense of responsibility, and it is this that Levin must eventually draw upon.

Before he has to rely on responsibility alone, Levin decides, out of love, to give up Pauline because she is suffering badly from the difficulties of having both a family and Levin. The deceits involved in the affair are becoming too fraught with danger: ". . . he had fled love to dispel her anxiety and misery. He had suffered to free her from suffering" (*NL,* 313). Malamud uses Levin's sacrifice to show his growth: relinquishing love paradoxically signifies a fuller understanding of love.

In a further reversal, she returns to Levin, saying that she will divorce Gilley and wants to renew their relationship. Levin now tries to regain the love that he drove out of himself to protect her. This somewhat absurd sequence seems designed to force Levin into the position of having to assess and reassess his basic values and emotions. Love becomes an intellectual exercise, one of fortitude and perseverance in the name of responsibility and morality. As Marcus Klein puts it: ". . . Levin will be a man who believes that ideals, as he says, 'give a man his value if he stands for them,' just as he will be a man for whom love is finally neither a joy nor an enrichment nor an emotional fulfillment, but a stern moral imperative" (Klein, 258).

As will almost always be the case in Malamud's writing, success for the protagonist is hedged with ambiguities. At one point Levin tells himself that he "had from the first resisted becoming her saviour, or victim" (*NL,* 346). Because of his desire to be a moral man, he is not sure which he is. In prosaic terms, he is making himself into her victim; in Malamudian terms, through becoming her saviour he is saving himself: "Throughout his fiction, the theme of victory through defeat is constant . . ." (Richman, 26). What is defeated is Levin's original concept of what his new life would constitute. His victory lies in a "mode of heroism that belongs with *The Assistant:* choosing to leave the way of the *luftmensh* and the liberal dreamer and take the path of submission and suffering . . . , the freedom to choose the absence of freedom" (Richman, 91–92).

In addition to having to change his idea of love from one of romance (love-making in a forest) to one of human responsibility—an acceptance of love as a burden rather than a lifting of the heart—Levin also must contend with the conflict inherent in his standing up for principle in the English Department while he is having an affair with the wife of one of his colleagues. Many critics have felt that the two plot strands are not related: that the Levin-Pauline strand and the Levin–English Department strand are mutually exclusive, one stressing Levin's personal development, the other his concern with issues of society and intellectual truth. However, because his relationship with Pauline eventually becomes one of personal responsibility as opposed to love, there is a strong parallel between the two aspects of the novel. Levin's stand against the department's policies also emanates from a strong sense of responsibility to higher values.

Levin takes action to resist the intellectual stagnation, fear, and censorship in the department both because of his belief in liberalism and on account of the changes that have occurred in him as a result of his experiences with Pauline: "Morality was a way of giving value to other lives through assuring human rights" (*NL*, 249). To Levin, morality does not consist of avoiding adultery, and he is aware of the moral shortcomings of this attitude. However, by demeaning Gilley as both a husband and an academic (Baumbach 1965, 105), Malamud tries not too subtly to justify Levin's actions. Morality becomes the acceptance of responsibility for "human rights"; responsibility to Pauline aids Levin in developing the courage to stand up for his beliefs in the department, and his trials in the department help him decide to sacrifice his future plans to the ideal of responsibility for an individual human being.

This is not a straightforward development, as each plot strand also serves to block the fruition of the other, creating a tension that Levin must resolve. He is aware that his affair with Pauline has gravely affected his ability to take a moral stance at the college. He thinks that if he were not involved with her, "He would not then have been incapacitated before her husband when there was an issue to fight for, a principle to defend . . ." (*NL*, 249). One critic rightly states that "Levin succeeds most hilariously and preposterously in changing himself much more than he succeeds in altering his environment" (Bluefarb, 76). In Malamud's writing it will always be the inner change of a character that is most important, even when that character is embroiled with social issues of great importance. Grappling with the moral issues involved in the conflict between private and public morality is what spurs Levin's growth and turns him into an ambiguously ethical man.

Levin sees his attraction toward Duffy as yet another instance of his being unable to extricate himself from his past of failure, but Duffy is really the only possible father figure that Cascadia will permit him to emulate and still remain a moral man, both Gilley and Fairchild being morally flawed. In fact, electing to follow Duffy's example of resistance to Cascadian norms leads Levin to moral success in Malamudian terms—that is, failure in the mundane world of the college, whose values are inadequate. This is a different type of failure than that which Levin experienced in the East, since there were no ethical kudos he could gain through his drunkard's life. Levin is wrong, therefore, in thinking that he is repeating past failures; his ambiguous, qualified success in Cascadia is of a completely different quality than anything he has experienced before.

It is not surprising that Duffy has also had a brief affair with Pauline, as Levin has become his alter ego. Levin's late knowledge of this affair causes him to wonder whether he is developing himself or simply following a pattern set by his unfortunate predecessor. Pauline chose Levin's photograph from a pile of applications on Gilley's desk; she called him across the continent. Levin thinks: "What she had probably wanted was someone like Duffy at a Duffyless time, so she settled for him come disguised with a beard" (*NL,* 311). He sees himself as "the extension of Duffy's ghost" (*NL,* 312), and he does, in fact, take up the fight where Duffy left it, succeeding more than Duffy did both personally (Duffy committed suicide) and in inspiring changes at the college. Thus Levin partially completes Duffy's work and vindicates his stance, despite the fact that he, as Duffy before him, suffers "expulsion from the new Eden of the West" (Ducharme, 66).

Levin's growth as a moral man reflects Malamud's idea of a writer's central purpose. Throughout the novel, Levin expresses opinions that parallel a remark Malamud made in 1958. Quoting Camus, he said, "'The purpose of the writer is to keep civilization from destroying itself.'"[5] Whatever shortcomings he may possess, Levin is primarily concerned with values that underlie civilization and with disseminating them to his students. Because of this concern, an important criticism of Levin is "his acceding to Gilley's demand that he abandon college teaching and thereby compromise the role of broader responsibility he had lately learned to shoulder" (Ducharme, 125).

At the end of the novel, Levin achieves a salvation of sorts by taking on responsibility for Pauline and her children. However, by abrogating his responsibility to future students and, by implication, to the wider humanity that they represent, he allows his personal needs—what he can salvage of his "new life" through Pauline, another human being—to overshadow his responsibilities to society. While he may show courage and inner growth in taking on the burden of Pauline in spite of Gilley's warnings concerning her shortcomings, Levin shares with the protagonists of *The Assistant* Malamud's qualified, ambiguous success: "'Even when it was right it was wrong' exactly describes Frank's position at the end of the novel, Levin's position at the end of *A New Life,* and Morris's whole existence" (Mandel, 265).

Form and Method

When Malamud was asked whether *A New Life* was derived from his experience teaching in the Northwest, he replied: "Let's say the switch from the East to the West suggested much of the material. . . ."[6] We have seen how important is Levin's view of the West from an Easterner's viewpoint.

Richard Astro, a member of the English Department at Oregon State, has commented on how "unendurable" would be the teaching, year after year, of four sections of composition in a "conservative and inflexible composition program."[7] Levin certainly finds it so with no literature "to ease the heart." Yet Malamud's own disenchantment with the English Department's program led Astro to comment that "there are just too many scenes and portraits in the novel which are mere personal justifications."[8] It would, of course, be a mistake to read the novel as mere autobiography, as Malamud felt that it is the imagination acting on events that makes effective writing. However, Levin expresses an overriding tone of negativity toward virtually everyone in the story. Far from perfect himself, he lacks the qualities that affect the reader's sympathies to quite the same extent as the Levin of Tolstoy's *Anna Karenina* with whom he shares a romantic ideal of nature. Seymour Levin finds it impossible to form any satisfactory relationships, though like Tolstoy's character he desires love, marriage, and a family. The heavy hand of the author is apparent.

A New Life is Levin's story. It is "principally about Levin's heroic destiny: his discovery of what it is and his acceptance of what it entails; the other characters, with the possible exception of Pauline (and Gilley at the end), are caricatures and stereotypes, part of the allegorical landscape of Levin's quest" (Baumbach 1965, 106). Levin does carry the stereotype of the city-bred Easterner ill at ease with Western customs and attitudes.

However, he also has traits that prevent him from becoming a pure stereotype. First, he is unsure of his own identity; he has five different first names in the course of the story. These names change from the anonymous S. Levin, which he brings from the East to obscure his full self, which is not really known to him; through Sy, what Gilley calls him, though the informality does not fit and does not succeed in making Levin one of the Cascadians, his past being too heavy a burden upon him (cf., sigh); to Seymour, as he slowly understands more about his own needs and principles and the ways in which these conflict with Cascadian norms; to Pauline's Lev (love), something he has desperately sought; and ending in Sam, which he says "they used to call me home" (*NL,* 350), thus bringing together a now accepted past with what will be his new life with Pauline.

Changes in the state of his beard also serve as signposts to change in Levin's conception of himself. Arriving bearded to change his face and hide what it formally was, he is, ironically, more conspicuous in Cascadia where all the men are beardless. Nadalee thinks he would be handsomer without it, and because of his need for a relationship he cuts off half an inch. He overhears a student discussing him as having "black whiskers" and being "nuts about some dame" (*NL,* 236). Later, to protect Pauline, he shaves off the beard completely, showing both his love for her and his ability to live with himself more easily, having shed at least some of his obsession with his past failures: "When Levin shaved his beard he symbolically indicted his willingness to expose himself to the shifting winds of time" (Ducharme, 112). Like his name changes, the state of Levin's beard serves a symbolic function.

Levin's name and Pauline's association of him with the Jewish boy she knew in college who was kind to her, makes it clear that he is Jewish. Yet, despite his being very probably the only Jew at the college or in the town, no one ever refers to this, though one critic thinks that "when Gilley tells him to go back to New York, he has something else in mind than its 'stinking subways.'"[9] While this is a possible interpretation of Gilley's remark, there is no particular evidence to support it. Although he would still be considered a Jew by those interested in looking for one, Levin has cut himself off from any Jewish past he might have had; at the least, any "'Jewish' elements in his thoughts and speech are suppressed" (Grebstein, 42). His liberal attitudes have as much to do with his New York upbringing as with any Jewish source, although Malamud presents his bad luck and blundering as aspects of the schlemiel / schlimazel character of Yiddish literature: a likable born loser or, in modern parlance, an antihero.

Despite Levin's apparent ease in fitting into the schlemiel / schlimazel mode, Malamud said: ". . . I don't much care for the schlemiel treatment of fictional characters. Willy-nilly, it reduces to stereotypes people of complex motivations and fates—not to mention possibilities" (Field 1975, 10). Expanding on this theme, he said elsewhere: "I have not given up the hero—I simply use heroic qualities in small men. Sometimes my characters do things so heroic that I myself blanch at their accomplishment" (Suplee, F8). He also felt that "a man who can overcome circumstances and his own weakness is not to me, a *schlemiel* . . ." (Tanner 1971, 329–30).

None of Malamud's remarks negate the possibility of seeing Levin as a schlemiel / schlimazel; they only cause us to question his particular definition of the term. The schlemiel can be defined, but his complexity is not removed. Isaac Bashevis Singer's Gimpel, for example, does not lapse into stereotype. Indeed, his approach to life's problems possesses great moral complexity, and he clearly illustrates the possibility of "heroic qualities in small men" and an extraordinary ability to "overcome circumstances and his own weakness." Malamud's idea of the heroic small man would not eliminate Gimpel—a schlemiel par excellence. Robert Alter observes that "to be a *schlemiel*—which, for Malamud, is almost interchangeable with the idea of being a Jew—means to assume a moral stance, virtually the only possible moral stance in his fictional world" (Alter 1970, 32).

The relationship between public and private moral stances is made clear. As Levin himself realized he cannot commit adultery with Pauline and resist Gilley's ideas in the department at the same time. Levin's ideas concerning liberalism retain their validity regardless of his actions with Pauline, but because his liberal ideals have the stature of moral principles, they lose validity and sincerity if he shows moral slackness in any area. Thus the two plot strands of ideals and morals are inexticably linked, as Gilley makes clear when he calls Levin a "false pretender to virtue" (*NL,* 328). The confrontation with Gilley is yet another example of how "the experience of failure in Malamud's fiction is simply the testing-ground of character; its purpose is to explore the possibilities for moral development and spiritual regeneration which follow from a recognition of the fact of failure."[10] It is Pauline who provides the source of one of Levin's most important failures: his discrediting in the English Department. It is also Pauline who makes possible his most important success: his awareness of the importance of selflessness and a real, if unexpected, new life.

A New Life uses social realism as its basic approach, with a strong element of satire. In *The Natural* and *The Assistant* realism had overtones of fable or parable. In *A New Life,* Malamud stays close to realism, in part through the use of a great deal of specific detail about the town, the college, and the people associated with both, but particularly the people associated with the college. Some critics feel that he fails to present Cascadia College or its people realistically, the staff being "a vague collection of academic types and stock grostesqueries" (Solotaroff, 247). I think this attitude is mistaken, as Malamud manages to present a convincing cross section of the staff and the issues at a small, rural, state college. The satire is at times biting, frequently passing over the line of humorous criticism; at that point it ceases to be satirical and becomes a polemic.

Malamud's realism is tempered by Levin's frequently romantic view of Cascadian nature and of his early relationship with Pauline. Clouds take on fantastic shapes, one "like a fat red salmon. Another was a purple flower. One was a golden-breasted torso out of Rubens" (*NL,* 162). Trees are seen in poetic terms: "White birches stood in baths of tiny yellow leaves. Elms had golden hair and naked black bodies" (*NL,* 123). In a 1963 interview, Malamud said that "through the use of every imaginative resource at the writer's command" the future novel would achieve "more than the merely realistic" (Richman, 48). Sidney Richman comments: "Malamud is a writer who has attempted to unite the realistic novel with the poetic and symbolic novel . . ." (Richman, 48).

Malamud also does not ignore the insights of naturalism. Levin is obsessed with the way the past impinges on the present, and he constantly fights what he sees as the deterministic quality of the past. Also, the pressures of Cascadian society create a straitjacket around action. Ultimately, however, both realism and naturalism must respond in Malamud's writing to an intangible human factor that goes somewhat beyond strict realism and beyond the determinism of naturalism; his characters can act to change what appeared to be fate.

Irony pervades the novel and is the basis of a good deal of its comedy. Time and again, attitudes Levin takes toward nature, teaching, and grandiose principles of liberalism are undercut by the reality of the situation or his own ineptitude and lack of understanding. He is a comic figure because things so often are and work out to be the opposite of what he expects. Because of the irony that is almost always present, any pity we might feel for Levin's plight as the prototypical outsider dissipates into humor or a sense of futility, a throwing up of the hands, given the sort of person that Levin is. The significance that the end of the novel gives to the title provides the ultimate irony: Levin's new life is extraordinarily different than anything he could have anticipated in the East.

A New Life is a college novel and has all of the shortcomings of that limited form. Noting that *A New Life* shows a decided expansion of theme over Malamud's previous two novels, Richard Astro observes that Malamud has attempted to create "a world large enough not only to carry his main themes of human connection, indebtedness and responsibility, but also able to sustain a love story, a Western adventure, a comedy, and a study of American academic life. But because the vehicle which Malamud chooses (the college novel) cannot support his tale of human suffering and regeneration, the novel ultimately fails" (Astro, 150). This problem is similar to the one Malamud encountered in *The Natural,* where the vehicle of baseball could not carry the weight of the themes imposed upon it.

Another problem in *A New Life* is the pace, which is very slow. Many of Levin's thoughts become repetitious and are less effective than the dream sequences that punctuate the tale and provide insight into his unconscious fears. The tone varies from the comic to the turgid, the grandiose and pompous to the pathetic. Because of the close relationship made between Levin's feelings, nature, and seasonal changes, the pathetic fallacy is much in evidence—though at times it is used quite effectively.

A New Life does not reach the level of artistic quality in *The Assistant,* although it does surpass that of *The Natural.* Many of the problems that Malamud encountered in his third novel he would overcome in his fourth, *The Fixer.* In particular, Malamud moves from a restrictive, academic setting that could not bear the weight of his themes, to one of suitable historical density that can provide a solid base a for tale fraught with moral, religious, and cultural complexities. In returning to a Jewish milieu, Malamud also finds a richer source of inspiration than he had had in *A New Life.*

Chapter Five
The Fixer

Historical and Social Background

The Fixer concerns the fate of Yakov Bok, a poor Jew in Tsarist Russia who undergoes great suffering during two-and-a-half years in prison. Malamud based the novel loosely upon the Mendel Beilis case.[1] I say "loosely" because much of what occurs in *The Fixer* has to do with things that are not part of the historical record; that is, Malamud focused on Bok's thoughts, his experiences in his cell, and his personal development as a moral human being. Malamud said that his father had told him the story of Mendel Beilis, and he recalled it forty years later when he wanted to write a novel concerned with injustice in America, spurred on in this direction by the Black rights movement. He stated:

> I use some of his [Mendel Beilis's] experiences, though not, basically, the man, partly because his life came to less than he had paid for by his suffering and endurance, and because I had to have room to invent. To his trials in prison I added something of Dreyfus's and Vanzetti's, shaping the whole to suggest the quality of the afflictions of the Jews under Hitler. These I dumped on the head of poor Yakov Bok. . . . So a novel that began as an idea concerned with injustice in America today has become one set in Russia fifty years ago, dealing with anti-Semitism there. Injustice is injustice.[2]

Malamud wanted to be able to invent, shape, and re-form the facts, the novel being "largely an invention. That is, I've tried to bring it as close to a folk tale as I could" (Field 1975, 10). Being a novelist rather than a historian meant that Malamud was interested in using what he called "imaginative fact" to create a "mythological quality": "I was dis-inventing history to give it a quality it didn't have.[3] This quality, partaking of imagination and myth, served to humanize the facts and permitted Malamud to strive for his goal of creating a work of art that would stress the heroic in a small man and, by implication, the essential value of all human beings. Thus, whereas Beilis was almost lost in the issues of his trial, Malamud, while certainly not permitting the wider implications of Bok's trial to be forgotten, forces our attention upon Yakov Bok the human being. It is noteworthy that the last line of the novel is, "Some shouted his name."[4]

Malamud sets Bok's development firmly within the exigencies of Russian history and the Jews within Russia, and within the much wider problem of the relationship of individuals and groups to historical movements. Yakov's attitude is that he is "not a political person" (*TF*, 54), something that will change by the end of the novel. All are affected by Russia's history of repression and by Nicholas II's fear of liberalization, as Bibikov, the investigating magistrate, confirms when he tells Yakov: "Russia is such a complex, long-suffering, ignorant, torn and helpless nation. In one sense we are all prisoners here" (*TF*, 187).

Malamud presents an accurate picture of the situation of the Jews in prerevolutionary Tsarist Russia. Shmuel tells Yakov that he is safer in the *shtetl* (Jewish village), as the Tsar "doesn't want poor Jews all over his land . . ." (*TF*, 18) and has, therefore, continued the use of the Pale of Settlement. In the large cities, Jews are restricted to a few districts— readily available for a pogrom; however, it is the poverty and lack of opportunity that eventually drives Yakov to look for work outside the district and to live in an area forbidden to Jews.

Malamud intertwines information about the historical setting with that relating to anti-Semitism and Christianity. There are a number of references to anti-Semitic folklore. Before Yakov even enters Kiev, the Dnieper boatman says that Jews have hooves (*TF*, 34), a reference to the belief among the bigoted masses that Jews are devils. A boy follows Yakov, "poking his fingers up like horns over his head . . ." (*TF*, 79) because the Bible stated that Moses had beams of light emanating from his forehead. Grubeshov tells Yakov that "in the Middle Ages Jewish men were said to menstruate" (*TF*, 101), a belief still held by some Russians, as the officials are waiting for Yakov to begin to bleed from his penis.

With popular beliefs like these, it is easy to understand how the blood libel (the belief that Jews murder non-Jews for ritual purposes) could still be accepted as fact despite, as Malamud points out, both popes and kings having stated that it was false, and the early Christians being called "blood drinkers" by the pagans (*TF*, 183). It is Christianity which Nicholas II and the Black Hundreds use to manipulate the population. Christian belief is strong, and anti-Semitism is rooted in Christianity. While it may be said that none of Bok's persecutors are true to their Christian faith (Bok asks Kogin, "How can anyone love Christ and keep an innocent man suffering in prison?" and Kogin answers, "There is no innocent Christ-killer . . ." [*TF,* 247]), it is all too easy to make Christianity serve the evil purposes of a fearful, reactionary, autocratic regime. It is noteworthy that Kogin will become Yakov's savior at the end of the novel, changed by his own sufferings because of his criminal son and able to sympathize with Yakov's sufferings in prison. Kogin's Christian faith may also have brought out his compassionate feelings: Yakov's reading to him from the New Testament may have had a positive effect.

Kogin is the exception; most Christians in the novel act in extraordinarily un-Christian ways. Malamud relies on the shock of hypocrisy to push home his attitude toward the perversion of religious belief. Thus Nikolai Maximovitch feels for the poor, cries over a dead dog, and praises mercy; however, he belongs to the Black Hundreds, who desire to murder people who happen to be Jews. The officials, particularly Grubeshov, are presented as nominal Christians but are clearly more concerned with matters of this world—with political considerations—than with the human implications of their religion. Grubeshov plans to use the "evidence of history" to help convict Bok. To Bibikov's comment that "history is not law," Grubeshov replies, "We will see about that" (*TF,* 138).

Father Anastasy presents the "historical evidence" for the ritual murder charge. His long lecture at the cave where Zhenia Golov's body was found sets out all the superstition, misinformation, and historical animosity toward Jews that provides the base for the blood libel. Upon that base, Grubeshov builds his fraudulent case. He adds to the blood libel the racial theories of the Comte de Gobineau and Houston Stewart Chamberlain, both nineteenth-century anti-Semites who propounded racist theories that excluded Jews from membership in the "Aryan race" and saw their very presence among European peoples as negative. Grubeshov sees the "Jewish Nation" as involved in a world conspiracy to overthrow the government of Russia and take over the country. The fears that constantly haunt the weak government of Nicholas II are clear from its embracing of these ideas, as is its desperation in trying to convince Yakov to sign a confession and not go to trial. The Tsarist government desires to focus the wrath of the population on the Jews in order to remove pressure from itself for long-needed reforms. Grubeshov predicts pogroms and massacres if Bok is acquitted. One of the results of this intense pressure is to make Yakov take upon his shoulders the historic destiny of the Jewish people.

Yakov thinks that "being born a Jew meant being vulnerable to history, including its worst errors" (*TF*, 164–65). He spends long hours trying to answer that most unanswerable of questions: Why me? He is forced to consider the relationship of the individual to historical forces, one of the central issues in the novel. These forces seem to be arbitrary and to affect everyone, but they are less arbitrary for Jews. Thus even Yakov's parents, who remained in the *shtetl*, so seeming to hide from history, were murdered as "historical necessity" caught them up: "If conditions were ripe whatever was likely to happen was waiting for you to come along so it could happen" (*TF*, 331).

Bok achieves some understanding of these forces through the philosophy of Baruch Spinoza, whose ideas also interest Bibikov. Bok is fascinated by Spinoza's view that "nature invented itself and also man. Whatever was there was there to begin with. . . . When it comes down to basic facts, either God is our invention and can't do anything about it, or he's a force in Nature but not in history" (*TF*, 272). If God is just a force in nature or is man's invention, Yakov can withdraw from any sense of involvement in Jewish history, since the idea that there is a special relationship between the Jews and God is a myth. Indeed, God can be seen as having nothing to do with man's history at all: it is totally within man's control to attempt to affect the flow of events.

By not depending on God, man is freed to act: "His study of Spinoza has taught him that history is Necessity, Fate, and Circumstance, but also that history can be altered, perhaps improved, by the free choices of men."[5] Much of Yakov's musings about Spinoza concern the extent of freedom possible if it is assumed that God has withdrawn from human concerns. When Bibikov asks him, "If a man is bound to Necessity where does freedom come from?" he answers, "That's in your thought, your honor, if your thought is in God. That's if you believe in this kind of God. . . . It's as though a man flies over his own head on the wings of reason, or some such thing. You join the universe and forget your worries" (*TF*, 85).

Though Yakov is impressed by the power of thought, he finds it impossible to use it effectively. Even Bibikov thinks that it is really only through politics that freedom can be achieved in any practical sense. Eventually Yakov also accepts that "personal freedom does not exist independently of the social and political order" (Desmond, 103). "Spinoza thought himself into the universe but Yakov's poor thoughts were enclosed in a cell" (*TF*, 220).

Yakov must move from the purely philosophical aspects of Spinoza's thought to the practical, to Spinoza's idea that it is the "purpose of the State to preserve a man's peace and security so he can do his day's work" (*TF*, 289). He becomes a political man; that is, someone who believes that he can affect historical circumstance through direct action: "What is it Spinoza says? If the state acts in ways that are abhorrent to human nature it's the lesser evil to destroy it" (*TF*, 352). Yakov has taken his understanding of Spinoza to revolution. This is much further than Bibikov had gone, for he thought that it was possible to work for change within a corrupt state, and he was destroyed because of his error.

Spinoza helps Yakov understand that while he cannot opt out of history, he need not—indeed must not—remain its passive victim. The Cossack who has his leg blown off is as much in history as Yakov is, but he has not gone through Yakov's process of understanding. He looks at Yakov "as though to say, 'What has my foot got to do with it?'" (*TF*, 348). This would have been Yakov's thought at the beginning of his imprisonment, however it no longer is, and because of this he has achieved a level of freedom that the Cossack lacks.

In his imagined confrontation with the Tsar, Yakov asks him why, with his experience of the hemophilia of his son, something that should have taught him compassion for others, he has "made out of this country a valley of bones. . . . You say you are kind and prove it with pogroms" (*TF*, 350–51). The Tsar denies responsibility; it is historical forces. What Yakov has learned through his experiences in prison and through Spinoza gives him the courage to imagine shooting the Tsar in the heart, the location of his greatest inadequacy. "As for history, Yakov thought, there are ways to reverse it" (*TF*, 352).

Suffering and Growth

Malamud has always believed in the possibility of moral growth. Indeed, this is a consistent theme in his fiction. He believes human beings to be capable of far better things than much twentieth-century ideology states. In his acceptance speech for the National Book Award for *The Magic Barrel*, in 1959, Malamud said, "I am quite tired of the colossally deceitful devaluation of man in this day. . . . Whatever the reason, his fall from grace in his eyes is betrayed by the words he has invented to describe himself as he is now: fragmented, abbreviated, other-directed, organizational. . . . The devaluation exists because he accepts it without protest" (Richman, 23).

Difficulties, obstacles, and suffering are what bring out in Malamud's characters their potential as human beings: "A bad reading of my work would indicate that I'm writing about losers. That would be a very bad reading. One of my most important themes is a man's hidden strength. I am very much interested in the resources of the spirit, the strength people don't know they have until they are confronted with a crisis."[6] This statement expresses the attitude Malamud takes toward Yakov Bok. He removes one support after another from him until Yakov has nothing to rely on but the resources of his own spirit. In the end, these resources prove sufficient to allow him to grow in human as well as historical understanding.

At one point during his imprisonment, Yakov "cursed history, anti-Semitism, fate, and even, occasionally, the Jews" (*TF*, 166). He will move from this position to a point of understanding history and fate, and becoming a sufferer for the Jews and for humankind rather than cursing them. He will learn to "shift resistance from suffering itself to those who impose it," realizing "that passivity is no good . . ." (Ducharme, 119). This will distinguish Yakov from previous Malamud protagonists in *The Assistant* and *A New Life,* because he has "never been the compliant and resigned sufferer that Morris Bober was or that Frank Alpine learned to be. He resisted his misfortunes with a stubbornness far beyond anything S. Levin was capable of. . . . The experience that taught other Malamud heroes to submit has taught Yakov Bok to resist" (Ducharme, 96). Like these three other characters, Yakov illustrates the value of suffering for other people; unlike them, but closest to Seymour Levin, he also learns the importance of resisting the causes of that suffering.

Yakov's moral growth occurs through the influence of his suffering on his views of the human condition, these views taking their most impressive form in his changing ideas on fatherhood. While he tells Bibikov that in his heart he is a father, he has already rejected both God and Shmuel, two father figures that have the possibility of providing a basis for a moral existence. He later tells Shmuel, reflecting Spinoza's influence, that God is nothing but a "force in nature but not in history. A force is not a father" (*TF*, 272). For moral growth to occur, Yakov, himself an orphan, must become a father in his heart and in actuality, not merely say that he is one. Becoming a father means that he will be responsible for the plight of other people and will have to extend his concern beyond himself, even to the extent of having an outgoing love for all of suffering humanity.

In reading the Hebrew Bible, Yakov becomes aware that "suffering . . . awakens repentance . . ." (*TF*, 254). Doubting that he can partake of this process, he realizes that he is concerned only with himself and his situation: "Nobody suffers for him and he suffers for no one except himself" (*TF,* 255). But a transformation does take place. Kogin, his guard, tells Yakov of his son Trofim who murdered an old man and will spend 20 years in Siberia. As a father Kogin grieves, and Yakov, touched by the suffering of a fellow human being, commiserates with him. Toward the end of the novel, Kogin saves Yakov's life, thereby sacrificing his own. He has become a father to Yakov, perhaps elevating him to his own lost son's place. As Tony Tanner suggests, Kogin, "in effect 'adopts' Yakov, just as Yakov 'adopts' Chaim. The found father himself finds a 'father'" (Tanner 1971, 336).

Yakov experiences a stunning insight, a type of epiphany, in which he extends himself beyond himself. He dreams that Shmuel is dead. Then, upon awaking, he says, "'Live, Shmuel,' he sighs, 'live. Let me die for you'" (*TF,* 287). He extends this feeling of responsibility to all the Jews: "He will protect them to the extent that he can. This is his convenant with himself" (*TF,* 228). Thus he gives his suffering meaning and his life purpose.

Yakov's full commitment to fatherhood and human responsibility occurs shortly after his dream of Shmuel. His wife Raisl visits him and asks that he write a note stating that he is the father of her illegitimate son, Chaim. He can respond to her weeping because "he had learned about tears" (*TF,* 303). She tells him that the man who fathered the child has left and is "not his father. Whoever acts the father is the father" (*TF,* 305). In accepting the role, Yakov shows that he has moved far beyond his earlier self-centeredness. In accepting Raisl and her child, he also confirms his sense of oneness with his people, as her name is an anagram for Israel.

The lawyer Ostrovsky tells Yakov, "You suffer for us all . . . ," and while Yakov's rejoinder is, "It's without honor. . . . It's a dirty suffering" (*TF,* 321), we have seen that his attitude toward his people has become one of responsibility and commitment. He has previously rejected a pardon that would have released him as a criminal and not as an innocent man. He wants a fair trial, not a pardon; he does not want the Jewish community to be pilloried by his false admission of guilt. Given his sufferings, this choice shows how much he has changed and is a telling comment on Malamud's faith in the common man and his capacity for moral growth. Tony Tanner observes that "the real trial is not a matter of sentence or acquittal but the imprisoned years which preceded it, during which a man has the chance to derive some meaning from what he is caught up in. It is in the prison, not in the courtroom, that a man must win his freedom and earn a new life" (Tanner 1971, 338).

Freedom in this novel, as in the previous three, consists of choosing selflessness over self-centeredness. In addition, in his dream of Bibikov, Yakov imagines the dead Investigating Magistrate telling him that "the purpose of freedom is to create it for others" (*TF*, 336). For Malamud freedom means not only the release from a literal prison but also, even more important, the release of caring and responsibility from the bars of selfishness. "Like S. Levin and Frankie Alpine, Bok must learn to sacrifice his physical freedom, his 'freedom to feel free,' as Levin puts it, in order to reach the spiritual, moral, and intellectual freedom he really seeks" (Cohen, 76).

In this same dream sequence, Yakov sees a crowd of prisoners:

> "Are you Jews or Russians?" the fixer asked them.
>
> "We are Russian prisoners."
>
> "You look like Jews," he said. (*TF*, 335)

He has now realized that prisoners are prisoners; they are indistinguishable in their suffering. Injustice affects all, Jews or not, and his moral stance as an innocent man who is made to suffer is for the benefit of humanity. This is an important further step in his moral development.

As stated, Yakov's moral development is directly related to his attitude toward fatherhood. He never establishes a relationship with God, but does come to view Shmuel—a Bober-like figure in his respect for the Jewish law and one who has a strong sense of God as father—as someone worthy of respect and love because of his simple human decency and his relation to the Jewish people. A parallel to the good-bad set of fathers is seen in Shmuel and God, and Bibikov and the Tsar. Indeed, Bibikov provides the clearest example of an acceptable secular father, one not committed to any religious creed but concerned for the welfare or humanity.

Bibikov places his faith in reformation of the Russian political system; he is a humanist and a liberal democrat. He asks Yakov how life could "be made better if not in politics or through it?" (*TF*, 87). As a supporter of Spinoza's ideas, he bolsters Yakov's contention that God cannot be depended on to make life better on earth; it is up to man to take seriously the political/social issues of society and to try to move repressive governments like the Tsarist state toward greater respect for human liberty. Alongside Yakov's moral growth moves his political growth: from stating, "I am not a political person" (*TF*, 54), he comes to believe that "there's no such thing as an unpolitical man, especially a Jew" (*TF*, 352). His suffering in prison, Spinoza, and Bibikov have combined to create this attitude.

On the way to his trial, Yakov has a hallucination in which he is talking to the Tsar whom he addresses at one point as "Little Father." Previously he had associated God directly with the evil Tsar: "The rod of God's anger against the fixer is Nicholas II, the Russian Tsar" (*TF*, 255). The two evil father figures conspire to persecute Yakov, the "suffering servant." That God could, in Yakov's mind, use Nicholas II as his instrument helps to support Yakov's negative conception of God. In the armored carriage, Yakov in his imagination discusses fatherhood with the Tsar, who appeals to his emotions with a description of his children, particularly the hemophiliac Tsarevitch, Alexis. To the Tsar's question, "Are you a father?" Yakov answers, "With all my heart" (*TF*, 349).

The Tsar's anguish over his son, and his stating that he loves his people and that though he must suppress the Jews for the good of the country, he wishes them well, does not impress Yakov, who clearly feels that the Tsar has learned nothing about suffering from fatherhood: "Excuse me, Your Majesty, but what suffering has taught me is the uselessness of suffering" (*TF*, 350). Unlike Yakov, the Tsar is not a father with all his heart.

While suffering is useless because of the pain it causes, clearly it has taught Yakov a great deal. His attachment to and feeling for people who suffer has grown from being virtually nonexistent at the beginning of the novel to the point where he sees himself as responsible for alleviating as much suffering as he can. His shooting the Tsar and, by association, God has been viewed by some critics as showing a lack of compassion. This is not so. His suffering has caused him to direct his compassion toward the mass of humanity who suffer injustice, and to desire to destroy those who cause it. When he says that he has changed, "I fear less and hate more" (*TF*, 336), this shows that he has ceased to be a passive recipient of injustice and become an active agent in resistance to it. He has learned to "love Raisl, whom he had hated, and to hate the Tsar, whose 'loyal subject' he had been."[7]

Malamud's treatment of the Tsar, if only in Yakov's dream vision, marks a turning point in his attitude toward patience in his characters: "The other Malamud heroes were satisfied with rejecting or displacing their ogre fathers. Bok is driven to destroy his symbolic false father, the Tsar . . ." (Ducharme, 96). The Malamud hero has become someone who will not tolerate a weak father when that weakness causes pain: "The Tsar is morally and emotionally atrophied, incapable of 'fathering' Russia or a healthy heir."[8] By contrast and paradoxically, Yakov, who has never actually fathered a child, is, because of his growth in compassion, a truer father than the Tsar, who is father to Alexis and putatively to Russia.

Sheldon Grebstein does not see Yakov as growing in love. He thinks that "hate for his tormentors sustains him much more than love for mankind. Where idealism does enter the novel, it appears only in glimmers" (Grebstein, 24). I find this idealism occurring far more often than in "glimmers" and that the stress of Yakov's growth is upon love for suffering humanity, his hatred being reserved for those that cause the suffering. He, like Frank Alpine before him, has learned "what Morris Bober knew—that each man suffers for other men, that everything relates underneath" (Cohen, 85). While he does not accept victimhood the way Morris and Frank do, Yakov shares certain qualities with them just as he diverges in others. It is the case that "Bok adds Frank Alpine's commitment to Bober-like endurance. . . . As with Bober, Bok's life is an endurance test whose only activity is suffering, but unlike Bober, Bok's actual imprisonment allows him to attain a spiritual freedom that eludes Bober" (Helterman 1978, 299). Not only does Yakov achieve this spiritual freedom, but he also moves beyond victim status in his belief that tyranny must be fought: "You can't sit still and see yourself destroyed" (*TF*, 352).

An important part of Yakov's growth into a man who feels responsibility toward others lies in his relationship to his own Jewishness, which, at the beginning of the novel, he rejects. Through the course of the novel, he reattaches himself to the Jewish people, their past and destiny. This provides a means whereby he can expand his feelings to include humanity as a whole, moving from the particular to the universal. As for his feelings about God, Yakov's attitude is that "He doesn't see us and doesn't care. Today I want my piece of bread, not in Paradise" (*TF*, 23). It is without great difficulty that he drops his prayer things into the Dnieper.

Malamud's heroes leave one place for another in an attempt to be rid of what they see as a restrictive past. Roy Hobbs, Frank Alpine, S. Levin, and Yakov Bok all fit this pattern. The problem is, they carry themselves with them, along with those elements of their past that they are so desirous of relinquishing; the past cannot be forsworn. Also, "the desire to escape the past serves as a metaphor for the flights from responsibility in the present" (Ducharme, 99). The characters must learn that happiness cannot be achieved while attempting to fulfill only themselves; concern for the welfare of others is essential for fulfillment.

Yakov's new life is built upon a denial of who he really is. To collect his reward, he agrees to decorate Lebedev's upstairs flat, without informing him that he is a Jew. This sin of omission he rationalizes by thinking, "After all it's only a job, I'm not selling my soul" (*TF,* 49). In fact he is, though it takes him some time to realize it. What he realizes soon after is that "he had stupidly pretended to be somebody he wasn't, hoping it would create 'opportunities,' had learned otherwise . . ." (*TF,* 80). Eventually, he sees that he cannot deny his Jewishness, as it is an inherent part of himself.

Yakov dreams of destroying his Jewishness when he envisions striking the Hasid on the head with a hammer; once he is arrested, Jewishness is forced upon him by the Russian state. In an attempt to distance himself from the *shtetl* and all it represents, he tells Bibikov that he is a Jew only by birth and nationality, but is now a "freethinker." Bibikov points out that the Russian state considers him a Jew. In saying that he is not ashamed of his fellow Jews, Yakov has already begun to defend them, even if only slightly. His admission that there are things about himself that he could be ashamed of shows that he is capable of seeing his own actions in some perspective; this bodes well for his future development. He rejects God, but not the Jews.

In the end what he believes in is the right of the Jewish people not to suffer merely because they are Jews, and Yakov extends his right to all of humanity. He puts on the cloak of the suffering Jew who suffers for the world. This can be seen in his attitude toward Shmuel, Raisl (Israel), and the Russian prisoners in his dreams. It is not by accident that Bok means goat, for Malamud has used Yakov as a representative of the Jewish people's historical role as scapegoat, expanding this to include him as a symbol and spokesman for suffering humanity. In Yiddish, Bok also means a piece of iron, and this meaning reflects Yakov's endurance. Shepsovich means son of a sheep. Yakov is, thus, a victim, but one who has within himself the ability to endure—like the Jewish people whom he symbolizes and the unjustly suffering for whom he speaks: "To be a Jew is to understand the suffering that God puts into the lives of all men. This understanding leads to goodness that must take the form of *rach-*

mones, pity, for other men, for other Jews, even for oneself" (Helterman 1985, 79).

Does Malamud present Yakov as a Christ figure in the sense of providing a vicarious redemption for the weak and oppressed? Iska Alter notes many parallels with the Jesus story in that Yakov is "a fixer, a carpenter who abandons his traditional community in his thirtieth year, in order to begin a new ministry among the godless; arrested in April during the Passover season; imprisoned with thieves and murderers; figuratively lost to the world; and even resurrected" (Alter 1981, 165). James Mellard remarks that "obviously, there is a great deal of irony in the use of such a 'Christ-figure' by a Jewish novelist, but Malamud's point in using it is to insist upon the universality of the pattern. . . ."[9]

Despite the similarities with the Christ story, there are closer references to Isaiah's suffering servant and to Job. Harold Fisch observes that Yakov "cannot quite see the point of redemption by suffering . . ." and has "moved away from the Christian reading of the 'suffering servant' chapters and has adopted something more like the traditional Jewish exegesis which sees the servant as the persona of the whole Jewish people, suffering the trials of its history."[10] While in one light, Yakov's suffering may be viewed as serving the purpose of improving Russian society and possibly even the world, within the purview of the Christian story, his own understanding of his role differs from this. He does not accept God's will but blames Him for his own suffering and for that of humankind, suffering that God could stop but chooses not to—a Job-like response. There is no sense of Yakov's accepting suffering as Jesus did, although Jesus feared it as would any man. "Bok resists to the end. Jesus advised his disciples not to resist the evildoer, to turn the other cheek to the enemy that had struck them. . . . Nothing could be further from the behavior of Yakov Bok" (Ducharme, 50), who dreams of shooting the Tsar.

Malamud stresses the resistant aspects of Job, those parts of his personality that refuse to accept God's will. At the end of the Book of Job, however, Job accepts God's judgment that he, a mere man, cannot expect to understand God's ways. No special meaning is given to his sufferings. This reflects Shmuel's approach to God, but not Yakov's. Elie Wiesel states that it is far from certain that Job was Jewish, but says that after his suffering, "If Job was not Jewish to begin with, he became Jewish."[11] Through his suffering, Yakov also becomes Jewish—in Malamud's symbolic use of the term as well as in his taking on of responsibility for the fate of the Jewish people. Suffering has given him an understanding of the plight of those who suffer.

Wiesel is offended by Job's ultimate surrender to God; he values most his resistance. In *The Fixer* Malamud also focuses on defiance. A major difference between Job and Yakov lies in the fact that Job never loses his faith in the existence and all-powerfulness of God, only in His goodness. Yakov often doubts God's existence because, unlike Job, he has never heard God speak to him nor seen any sign of his favor. For Yakov, God may not be all-powerful and is certainly not good. Both characters feel that they are suffering unjustly and want answers from God that He refuses to give.

Unlike Jesus, Yakov adopts a very this-worldly approach to salvation—very much a Jewish rather than a Christian approach—that is concerned with social justice here and now rather than with its achievement in heaven. This approach is suggested in the Book of Job as well, in that there the concern is with justice on earth, the idea of divine reward and punishment in an afterlife not yet having been developed in Jewish thought when the book was composed. If there is any comparison possible between Yakov and Jesus, it is only on the basis that both suffer in an unjust world. Even so there is a problem in that Jesus saw himself as doing the will of an ultimately benevolent Father, whereas Yakov finds it impossible to accept such a being, given the injustices and horrors of the world. He grows in ways that he could not have predicted at the beginning of the story, but that we as readers might have, given the direction of Malamud's previous novels.

Form and Content

While critical reaction to *The Fixer* was mostly very positive, some readers found its descriptions of human misery and physical brutality offensive. Philip Roth for example, called the novel "a relentless work of violent pornography. . . ."[12] I share the opinions of those who saw the novel in a highly positive light, and judge it, along with *The Assistant,* as a novel that firmly establishes Malamud's reputation as a major American writer. Roth's observation seems to me idiosyncratic, particularly because neither the Marquis de Sade nor Pauline Reage, the author of *The Story of O,* both of whom Roth compares with Malamud, are concerned with issues of compassion, human dignity, or unjust suffering. Malamud himself said, "I wanted to write a gutsy, triumphant book, not a book about defeat and sorrow. I was writing about a folk hero. I was trying to move from history to mythology. The actual trial was an anticlimax. I couldn't possibly use it. The book nearly killed me—but I couldn't let go of it."[13] He went on to state that he wanted to defend the human, to "explicate life." What attracted him to the subject was its drama.

The influence of Dostoyevski in this novel is strong. Overtones of his writing can be seen in Malamud's description of a Tsarist prison and of its guards and criminal inmates. Malamud's major debt to the great Russian novelist lies in his stress upon suffering, which was central to Dostoyevski's vision of human life. There is a difference, however, in the two authors' approach, in that "where Dostoyevski holds suffering to be a means of purification and salvation, Malamud treats it as an inexorable affliction to be endured with dignity and resolution. . . . Like Dostoyevski, Malamud believes shared anguish should lead to mutual sympathy and brotherhood. But he rejects the Russian's conviction that men are innately vicious and cruel."[14] This is in stark contrast to Philip Roth's implications.

The Fixer contains overtones of folklore, particularly that seen in the work of such Yiddish writers as Sholem Aleichem, I. L. Peretz, and Isaac Bashevis Singer. Stylistically, Yakov's speech is unsophisticated and often earthy, containing Yiddish proverbs and idioms. His attempts at self-education through reading books he barely understands add the thinnest patina of abstract thought to his simple speech. Malamud's admitted debt to Hemingway can be seen in Yakov's spare sentences and the descriptions of his endurance in prison. While it cannot be called "grace under pressure"—the last thing Yakov does is accept his suffering gracefully—his very tenacity, his refusal to sign a confession even upon offers of freedom, has Hemingwayesque qualities, although this refusal has more altruism in it than can be found in Hemingway's characters.

There are also influences on the novel from the Jewish history of survival and endurance over the centuries and from the Hebrew Bible, particularly from Yakov's namesake Jacob. Like the biblical Jacob, Yakov comes to symbolize the Jewish people, both fulfilling Jacob's prefiguration of the exiled Jew and serving as a twentieth-century symbol of one. As Jacob eventually marries Rachel, so Yakov eventually accepts Raisl as his true wife.

Malamud said, "I would never deliberately flatten a character to create a stereotype. . . . Most of all I'm out to create real and passionate human beings. I do as much as I can with a character" (Field 1975, 16). A number of critics have felt that Malamud did not do enough with his characters in *The Fixer*, however, focusing all his attention on his protagonist. A frequent criticism is that the other characters serve merely as foils for Yakov, to clarify or illustrate his situation or views. The secondary characters are often felt to be too flat, tending on occasion to "degenerate into schematic caricatures, thus weakening the inner logic of the narrative (e.g., the anti-Semitic owner of the brick factory, policemen, priests, and several others are each endowed with a single dominant trait, like the heroes and villains of neoclassical drama)."[15]

This accusation is not entirely fair; as in any novel, the characters range from fully rounded to partially formed to flat. As the protagonist, Yakov of course receives the fullest treatment, but many other characters are very far from being flat, cardboard figures, including Shmuel, Bibikov, Zina Lebedev, Marfa Golov, and even Kogin. They contribute to our understanding of Yakov and also possess clear personalities of their own that give them a limited complexity. The one-dimensional characters, such as Grubeshov, Father Anastasy, Raisl, and Ostrovsky, to name a few, more clearly serve as extensions of Yakov and his plight. Yet even Yakov's imagined Tsar has more substance than is at first consideration apparent.

Malamud gives his characters a number of different language styles in the novel. The reader must remember that Yakov speaks to other Jews in Yiddish and thinks in it as well. He must use Russian in communicating with non-Jews. The ferry man has difficulty in recognizing his accent and assumes he is a foreigner; Nikolai Maximovitch tells him, "You speak well although with a provincial accent. But grammatically" (*TF,* 46); and Proshko asks, "Why is it you talk Russian like a Turk?" (*TF,* 66). The main difference between Yakov's Yiddish and his Russian on the page is Malamud's use of Yiddish proverbs and idioms and an occasional inverted word order for the Yiddish. The Russian he presents in ordinary, good prose.

Other language includes that of the indictment, a legal prose stilted and remote from the horrendous matters it describes, and the formal syntax of the officials, which contrasts with Yakov's simpler, natural speech: "Accordingly, there is posed the repeated incongruity between what is uttered by the various magistrates and functionaries, and the pithy, unaffected quality of what Yakov is saying inside his own head. The incongruity becomes even more absurd in that when Yakov replies to his persecutors, he usually does so in the same stilted manner they use" (Grebstein, 42).

The novel is written in a naturalistic style: Yakov must try to cope with events and forces—history—beyond his control. As we have seen, however, there are choices that he can make within the world, and because he does have some choice, this is not pure naturalism (if such a form exists). Malamud depicts the victory of the human spirit over the forces of darkness by using an omniscient third-person point of view that focuses entirely on Yakov's inner life. The device "reinforces the claustrophobic atmosphere of the novel. This is the formal equivalent to the action, which consists largely of Yakov's experiences in solitary confinement" (Grebstein, 35).

Through the use of an omniscient point of view, Malamud is able to range over all the subtleties of Yakov's changing thoughts and feelings, the elucidation of which is central to Malamud's approach. What happens in the world outside Yakov's cell and psyche filter in to him piecemeal and is of lesser importance than what he makes of the information. Malamud succeeds in setting Yakov against external facts but tries to "allegorize the inside, putting the central character symbolically against himself."[16] It is this internal struggle that is at the heart of the novel.

The historical setting and Malamud's attention to detail help to create the sense of realism that pervades the novel. Some of the detail, however, is not based upon fact; this is, after all, a work of fiction. Critics have stated, for example, that Tsarist prisons were not quite as bad as Malamud presents them. Also, the title of the novel comes from an unlikely source outside the story's time and place. Malamud said, "The title— once you make it part of a Russian setting, it becomes almost a Russian word, yes? Well, it came to me in Corvallis, Oregon. . . . There was a sign I would see almost every day—'Jim the Fixer.' That's where the title came from . . ." (Frankel, 40).

Malamud does not rely on realism alone to tell Yakov's story: "I thought that if I could make the fantasy world real, then I could make Yakov's world real" (Frankel, 40). The longer Yakov remains imprisoned, the more blurred are his distinctions between fantasy and reality. Dreams and hallucinations become Yakov's method of confronting figures like the Tsar, whom he can approach in no other way. Characters directly involved in his persecution (Marfa Golov, Grubeshov, even Zhenia) also figure prominently in these visions, which become increasingly aggressive and brutal. Since he is walled off from the real world, he creates his own reality, and since we see everything filtered through his mind, Yakov's reality greatly affects the reader's sense of what is true.

As Yakov's perceptions are at the center of the novel and make up its most important aspect, Malamud's use of dreams, visions, and hallucinations constitutes a valid structural device that focuses attention not on the outside world but on the fixer's inner one: ". . . the dreams illustrate the major thematic conflicts between right and wrong, and they highlight the significant motifs and symbols that run throughout the narrative, helping to unify it. More important still, through the dreams we see the new Bok emerging . . ." (Sant, 178). Because his dreams and hallucinations reflect both his conscious and unconscious mind, the true state of the tortured protagonist comes to the fore when we see him trying to understand in dreams issues that he cannot cope with when awake or "conscious."

While *The Fixer* is set within a particular place and historical period, there are many foreshadowings of the Holocaust. Malamud uses the persecution of one Jew to illustrate the societal attitudes that support such action and that would lead to the murder of millions of equally innocent people. Perhaps this is the only way a fiction writer can come to grips with an event of such magnitude—by focusing on one victim of injustice. Malamud shows that within Tsarist Russia exist all the prejudices held by Nazi Germany, beginning with the ferryman's prediction of the mass slaughter of the "Zhids" and the burning of their corpses in "fires that people will enjoy all over the world. . . . You can take my word—the time's not far off when everything I say, we will do . . ." (*TF*, 35).

There are numerous references to the chimneys in the brick works, as when Yakov dreams that one of the workers, Richter, "carrying a huge black bag on his back, was following him down the road by the graveyard. When the fixer turned to confront the German and asked him what he was carrying in the bag, the driver winked and said, 'You'" (*TF*, 72). He dreams of a pogrom carried out by cossacks, and later says to Shmuel, "We're dealing nowadays with the slaughter of large numbers and it's getting worse" (*TF*, 273), the Jews finding themselves "in a black and bloody world. Overnight a madman is born who thinks Jewish blood is water" (*TF*, 288). Near the end of the novel there is a final image that imprints itself on Yakov's mind: "Then as they passed the brick wall of a factory, its chimneys pouring out coal smoke . . . he caught a reflected glimpse of a faded shrunken Jew in the circle of a window . . ." (*TF*, 345). Malamud said that "the afflictions of the Jews under Hitler . . ." constitute one of the burdens that he placed upon Yakov's head. Malamud reaches into the future to add to the impact of his tale of the innocent suffering, and awareness of the slaughter that will occur thirty years from Yakov's time affect one's reading of his plight.

In each of his novels through *The Fixer,* Malamud presents a protagonist who must eventually realize that the only way to achieve self-respect and a measure of freedom is through selflessness and acceptance of responsibility for the needs of others. Roy Hobbs, Frank Alpine, Seymour Levin, and Yakov Bok all have to learn this lesson. Though he learns it too late, Roy does beat up the Judge and Gus and reject the bribe. Frank refuses to accept his fate and uses the Bober store to discipline himself in selflessness. Levin becomes political in his attempt to change the English Department, and takes responsibility for Pauline and her children. Yakov grows in compassion and finally no longer thinks solely of himself. Also, as Robert Ducharme argues, Yakov resists his suffering more strongly than do the other protagonists. Malamud retains his belief in the usefulness of suffering for changing people. In the four novels discussed so far, this change is for the better. He has, however, made it clear that he does not like suffering, and in *The Fixer* he has Yakov resist it to the point of dreaming of murder and revolution—no passive resignation here. It should be noted, though, that all of Malamud's protagonists sooner or later resist their fate; it would be wrong, for example, to consider Frank totally passive, since he battles to change himself, although he settles for a life that Yakov would certainly reject.

In his next novel, *Pictures of Fidelman,* Malamud moves the setting to Italy and is concerned with the growth of a would-be artist, a comic picaro. Stylistically and thematically, this opens new doors for him.

Chapter Six

Pictures of Fidelman: An Exhibition

Style

Pictures of Fidelman: An Exhibition is not merely a collection of unrelated short stories. It is a book comprising stories that can both stand on their own and serve as fully fledged chapters of a novel (what Forrest L. Ingram calls "a short-story cycle").[1] A complication in this plan is that Malamud decided to compose the novel after having completed the first piece, "The Last Mohican," in 1957. As a result, the first story does not cohere with the other five as closely as they do with each other. Nonetheless, "Last Mohican" introduces many of the themes that pervade the work, setting the tone and introducing two characters, Fidelman and Susskind, who provide much of the book's unity.

In a letter to Robert Ducharme in 1970, Malamud stated that he saw the book as "a loose novel, a novel of episodes, like a picaresque piece" (Ducharme, 129). In two interviews given five years later, Malamud expanded on his earlier remark: "Right after I wrote 'The Last Mohican' in Rome in 1957, I worked out an outline of the other Fidelman stories, the whole to develop one theme in the form of a picaresque novel. Why do it the same way all the time? I used my mother's maiden name because I needed a name I liked" (Field 1975, 14–15).

After the first story, Malamud had an overall pattern of development of theme and character in mind. Also, he wanted to experiment, to try a fictional form new to him: ". . . I jotted down ideas for several incidents . . . I was out to loosen up—experiment a little—with narrative structure. And I wanted to see, if I wrote it at intervals—as I did from 1957 to 1968—whether the passing of time and mores would influence his life. I did not think of the narrative as merely a series of related stories because almost at once I had the structure of a novel in mind and each part had to fit that form" (Stern, 58–59).

The form of the book is not unique. Among others, Sherwood Anderson's *Winesburg, Ohio* and William Faukner's *The Unvanquished* both use short stories instead of traditionally structured chapters. As in *Pictures of Fidelman,* their stories develop common themes and use certain characters throughout to create unity and coherence. Like *Winesburg, Ohio, Fidelman* is a *Bildungsroman,* a novel that traces the education and development of a character. Unlike Anderson's novel, it is also a *Künstlerroman,* a novel tracing the development of an artist. There are parallels to James Joyce's *A Portrait of the Artist as a Young Man* in the book's title, in the title of the fifth story ("Pictures of the Artist"), and in the pattern of moral growth experienced by both protagonists—Arthur Fidelman and Stephen Dedalus.

One critic even compares the novel to *Adventures of Huckleberry Finn,* "in that we have a combination of two subgenres: the *Picaresque* and *Bildungsroman:* i.e., the one portraying the episodic, seemingly indiscriminate movement of a character from place to place, and the other showing the growth of a central character amidst swirls of experience. In Malamud all is infused with the comic tone. . . ."[2]

The picaro is a type of character who must create his own identity, create his life from a plethora of experiences. The Malamud picaro, Fidelman, has numerous characteristics of a schlemiel, and many critics have seen him as such. Unquestionably, Fidelman displays schlemiel-like traits: he is a hard-luck person who refuses to accept the truth of his inability to succeed as a painter. He tries again and again, failing constantly, seemingly unable to change his behavior. He is a bungler, whose failures are presented in a comic manner. He possesses neither judgment nor luck and, while being likable, has, until the final tale, all the traits of a born loser.

Malamud did not view Fidelman as a schlemiel, however. When asked if Fidelman was characterized as one, he answered, "Not accurately. . . . He does better. He escapes his worse fate. I dislike the schlemiel characterization as a taxonomical device. I said somewhere that it reduces to stereotypes people of complex motivations and fates. One can often behave like a schlemiel without being one" (Stern, 59). Despite this statement, it is difficult to remove Fidelman from the company of schlemiels who populate Jewish-American literature and, indeed, appear regularly in Malamud's novels and stories. At the conclusions of "Last Mohican" and "Glass Blower of Venice," the first and last stories in the book, he does show the morality that so many classic schlemiel figures illustrate. That morality is lacking in the middle four tales, a fact which, along with his eventual "success" as a man and a craftsman, does remove him somewhat from the traditional schlemiel. However, it is not sufficient to override the basic elements of his characterization.

The book is unified as a novel not by a consistency of narrative style but by the centrality of Arthur Fidelman in each tale/chapter, with all issues seen as they impinge upon him. Italy does provide a common setting, though the cities differ (Rome, Milan, Florence, Naples, and Venice). Another unifying factor is the recurring concern in each tale with matters of art. The book's subtitle, "An Exhibition," relates to the way in which each story "exhibits" a different aspect of Fidelman's development and shows how, in each, "Fidelman pursues a different kind of artistic endeavor . . . and loses a different part of his American values" (Helterman 1985, 132). Furthermore, Tony Tanner observes that each tale "has some subtle connections with particular painters or paintings—Giotto, Rembrandt, Titian, Picasso, Modigliani, Tintoretto" (Tanner 1971, 340). Finally, there are references to Susskind in four of the six tales. Either he is an actual character, or he exists as a demanding vision in Fidelman's mind.

Although there exists a coherence between all six tales, it is particularly evident in the final three: "I can say without reservation that the last three stories were written in a short time of each other because I saw the book as a picaresque novelistic whole and wanted to complete it" (Ducharme, 132n). His desire to complete the work impinged upon Malamud's stated aim to write it at intervals in order to see whether time changed his vision of Fidelman. The last three stories were published within two years of each other in 1968 and 1969.

Malamud said, "My novels are close to plays. I had once, as young writer, wanted to be a playwright" (Field 1975, 13). Each story in *Fidelman* clearly places the protagonist in a different situation that tests his character, moral development, and artistic growth, and it is easy to see how the tales can be viewed as scenes as well as portraits, as the novel possesses a strong theatrical quality. In Fidelman's movements about Italy, there is also a Jamesian international theme. Fidelman is a comparative innocent among the more worldly and mature Italians, although unlike James's Americans abroad, he lacks overall moral superiority.

The tone of *Fidelman* is largely comic, with the protagonist's experiences giving rise to various types of low comedy, including farce and slapstick. There are also examples of high comedy and wit and of satire, particularly in Malamud's burlesque of art through his focus on the talentless artist, Fidelman.

There is a great variety of diction and syntactical structures in the book, from slang and vernacular language to the jargon of high art. Malamud frequently mixes the diction for comic effect. He also uses various points of view. The third-person omniscient author predominates, and there is much interior monologue, particularly in "Pictures of the Artist," which is the most unconventional and surrealistic of the tales. Tenses change from past to present and back to past, reflecting the influence of the past on Fidelman's attempts to come to grips with life and art. In its variability and constant movement—the changes from rhetorical to colloquial, past events to present ones, straightforward narration and dialogue to interior monologue, serious literalness to comic irony, and references to great artists and to Fidelman's own artistic efforts—the style mirrors the basic conflict in the novel between the ideal and reality, between what Fidelman wishes was the case to what actually is.

Art and Life

Although *Pictures of Fidelman* is largely concerned with the development of a man and a would-be artist, the first story, "Last Mohican," also focuses on the issues of Jewish identity, something that either disappears completely or is far from being a central issue in the following tales. Thus it shares with *The Assistant, The Fixer,* and many of Malamud's stories a theme that has invigorated some of his best fiction and that connects him with a number of other Jewish-American authors. In this story, the identity problem relates directly to Fidelman's relationship to his Jewishness; in later Fidelman stories, the problem will be broadened to rest upon his conception of himself as an artist and a man.

Shimon Susskind symbolizes one half of Fidelman's self, a half that he would like to forget through assimilation. Fidelman's resistance to Susskind's demands reflects a desire to take on a new past: that of Italy and Italian art, Giotto in particular. As befits an essential part of Fidelman, Susskind sees him for what he really is: "'I knew you were Jewish,' he said, 'the minute my eyes saw you.' Fidelman chose to ignore the remark."[3] Susskind will force Fidelman not merely to pay attention to his remark but to live up to his name—faithful man—and, through causing him to suffer, to take upon himself the burden of his Jewishness through responsibility for the wandering refugee whom he would deny. The thematic parallel to Malamud's previous novels is clear: moral growth occurs through suffering and a selfless attitude toward others.

We are told that Fidelman is a "self-confessed failure as a painter . . ."

(*PF,* 3) and has decided to become an art critic. Susskind relates Fidelman's attempts to ignore his heritage with his failure as a critic who must grasp the intricacies of a foreign heritage. Voluntarily detached from his own past, he cannot write insightfully about another's because he lacks comprehension of the soul, the essence, of what a meaningful heritage infuses into a work of art. An understanding of life, of the importance of sympathy and human compassion, is a prerequisite for insight into art as either painter or critic. Ihab Hassan observes that in "Last Mohican" "Malamud had made grotesquely clear the triple failure of his hero: as painter, as art critic, and as *mensch.*"[4] The story will pursue Fidelman's growth as a human being—a mensch—success in art being of secondary importance.

Through Susskind, Malamud puts pressure on Fidelman in the areas of art, identity, and human compassion and responsibility. Fidelman's growing understanding of who he really is and of what his responsibilities are to Susskind, a suffering human being, plays a central role in causing him to give up his dream of becoming an art critic. As one commentator writes, "In reality it is more important that Fidelman find Susskind than his Giotto manuscript" (Cohen, 94). Susskind has, in fact, done him the favor he says he did when he destroyed the manuscript; he has forced him to try to find Susskind himself, and this search forces Fidelman to come to a realization of what Susskind symbolizes—his own Jewishness and a needy recipient for his compassion.

Susskind is frequently running, and when Fidelman asks him where from, he answers, "Where else but Germany, Hungary, Poland? Where not?" (*PF,* 7). He is the archetypal Wandering Jew, and in the first half of the story it is he who pursues Fidelman, who, after their first meeting, "certainly never thought of him . . ." (*PF,* 12). After the theft of his Giotto manuscript, Fidelman thinks of him a good deal and begins pursuing him. He dreams of Susskind and associates his search for him with Jewish images: the Jewish catacombs and a seven-flamed candelabra. At the police station, he places a value of 10,000 lire on his stolen pigskin briefcase, but "for 'valore del manoscritto' he drew a line" (*PF,* 23). He is learning the value of things, Susskind having "the power to lead Fidelman in and out of dreams and then out of himself toward God" (Helterman 1985, 127). Susskind is not quite a supernatural figure, though he does possess elements of one in his ability to appear without explanation and in his heavily symbolic role.

We are told that Fidelman "was lost without a beginning" and "needed something solid behind him before he could advance, some worthwhile accomplishment upon which to build another" (*PF, 25*). This reference to his stolen manuscript also refers to his Jewish heritage, which is "the real missing chapter of his own past, of himself."[5] His pursuit of Susskind leads him to the Jewish present and past. He searches in a synagogue, the Rome ghetto, and the Jewish cemetery, where Susskind prays for the dead. After visiting Susskind's "freezing cave" of a room, Fidelman is changed, ". . . from the visit he never fully recovered" (*PF, 35*). He no longer sees Susskind as a schnorrer but as a suffering human being. After Fidelman offers him his other suit freely, not expecting anything in return, Susskind returns the briefcase, having burned the chapter because of its inadequacy.

It is during his final attempts to catch the refugee, to "cut your throat," as he says, that Fidelman, "moved by all he had lately learned, had a triumphant insight" (*PF, 37*). If his insight is interpreted only in terms of "Last Mohican" and not with a view to the tales that follow, then Fidelman's epiphany signifies his achievement of a secular redemption: "'Susskind, come back,' he shouted, half sobbing. 'The suit is yours. All is forgiven'" (*PF, 37*). While he never actually catches Susskind, Fidelman has learned the importance of his Jewish heritage, of human compassion, and of his inadequacy as an art critic. His moral growth is clear.

His insight takes on a different meaning, however, when it is seen as pointing toward the second story, "Still Life." Robert Ducharme observes that "when the two stories are read as parts of a related sequence, one discovers in retrospect that Fidelman's triumphant insight had more to do with art than with life and that it was no triumph but a mistake" (Ducharme, 129). Fidelman realizes that he has no ability as an art critic and decides in "Still Life" to attempt again to be a painter. Because "Last Mohican" was not originally seen as the first section of what would become a novel, it is, as mentioned earlier, distant in some respects from the five other stories. I think that Fidelman's "triumphant insight" is best read as moral growth and accepted responsibility toward Susskind, with all that Susskind has come to symbolize in "Last Mohican." The view linking it principally with "Still Life" exposes an unfortunate seam that Malamud was unable to stitch together.

"Still Life" shows Fidelman having reattached himself to the goal of becoming a painter. There are threads relating back to "Last Mohican," as Fidelman's painting is adversely affected by his knowledge of art history: "Since he had always loved art history he considered embarking on a 'Mother and Child,' but was afraid her image would come out too much Bessie—after all, a dozen years between them. . . . A curse on art history—he fought the fully prefigured picture . . ." (*PF*, 48). Just as in "Last Mohican," where Fidelman lacked an acceptance of his tradition and so could not grasp the essence of Giotto's painting and become a successful art critic, so in "Still Life" he again fails to use tradition creatively, seeing it only as a burden. Even his own family (his sister Bessie) fails to provide a secure base from which he can launch himself into creativity.

At one point, he attempts to use what he has learned about his Jewish heritage: "Almost in panic he sketched in charcoal a coattailed 'Figure of a Jew Fleeing' and quickly hid it away. After that, ideas, prefigured or not, were scarce" (*PF*, 48). Susskind still haunts him, but Fidelman cannot cope with what he symbolizes in relation to his Jewish heritage and the plight of suffering individuals. This lends support to the interpretation that his "triumphant insight" had more to do with art than with an understanding of his own past and with humanity. As one critic comments: "In 'Still Life' Fidelman's fear of painting Susskind leads him to paint abstractions until he reaches the ultimate, a blank canvas" (Ducharme, 137). He tries to convince himself that even a canvas with nothing on it has value for the "painter." In fact, not painting reveals more about Fidelman than he realizes; a blank canvas describes his ties to his past as well as his present state as a painter and his future prospects as one. Iska Alter observes that "Fidelman's ambiguous failure is indicated by the story's title: 'Still Life,' a representation chiefly of inanimate objects, suggesting not only the promise of survival but also implying death-in-life . . ." (Alter 1981, 130).

In an attempt to ingratiate himself with Annamaria, his landlady, Fidelman imitates her method of beginning each painting with a religious symbol—crosses for her, a Star of David for him. This does not show any increase in his religiosity or attachment to his Jewish roots but is merely a comically cynical way of attempting to get her into bed. Similarly, in his desperation to find a paintable subject, he considers among others, "nude gray rabbis at Auschwitz . . ." (*PF*, 54). The lack of a heartfelt desire to paint any specific subject, in particular the apparent lack of any emotion in regard to the rabbis at Auschwitz, reveals the exploitative nature of Fidelman's character which, because of his lack of artistic talent, relies on sheer expediency.

Fidelman reaches a point where he can only paint himself, a clear sign of his limitations as both a man and an artist, and Annamaria is surprisingly similar to Fidelman in her limitations. Fidelman recognizes that she is a bad artist and that she has great problems in sorting out her life, her love life being nonexistent and her religious beliefs immersed in superstitions " 'Eh,' she shrugged, 'who can explain art.' Thus Malamud introduces the major theme of the story, the relationships between art, religion, and life. . . . She uses either art, religion or life as means to reach each of the others. None should be the means to an end. This fact is what Fidelman must learn" (Cohen, 97).

The sexual finale in the story merely illustrates how far Annamaria has yet to travel before her ability to cope with religion and life is any different than her understanding of art. As for Fidelman, at the end of this tale we see him as a failure in painting, religion, and life. In "Still Life" he is a prisoner to his lust for Annamaria; in "Naked Nude," the next story, he will be a prisoner to brutal men. The theme of imprisonment is a constant one in Malamud's writing.

At the beginning of "Naked Nude" Fidelman absently draws a hanging figure: "Who but Susskind, surely. A dim figure out of the past" (*PF*, 70). Although Fidelman refers to the hanging Susskind as a friend, the drawing connotes either the desire to destroy the man and what he symbolizes or the fact that Fidelman has already succeeded in doing so. However, the fact that he has drawn him shows he has not excised Susskind's image from his mind. Indeed, a second drawing depicts what is probably another attempt at removing Susskind from his unconscious: "A long-nosed severed head bounces down the steps of the guillotine platform" (*PF*, 70). In the midst of his imprisonment, Fidelman cannot take any comfort from his initiation into his heritage and sense of human compassion, to which he was exposed in "Last Mohican."

After he is reduced to cleaning toilets and running errands in a brothel, Fidelman's life as a painter takes an unexpected turn when he becomes not an artist but a copyist. His attempts to copy Titian's *Venus of Urbino* lead him into his own past, something he would rather avoid. His mind constantly dwelling on nudes, he dreams of his sister taking a bath as he, age 14, spies on her through the keyhole. As in "Still Life," the confusion and guilt caused by this entwining of mother and sister (Fidelman is aware that he had lusted after Bessie as he later would after Annamaria), has prevented him painting the *Venus*. Eventually he is able to transmute his lust into love for the *Venus* and copying Titian's masterpiece becomes not so much a quasi-artistic exercise as an attempt to fill a gap in his love-starved life.

His copying brings forth both feelings of love and artistic integrity, which is ironic in that he is creating a forgery. Ben Siegel has written that

"Malamud's goal in these stories, he has stated, is to have his comic hero 'find himself both in art and self-knowledge'" (Siegel, 126). His attitude toward art becomes highly ethical the more he works on his copy. When he is about to begin the painting, Fidelman has second thoughts, since he sees what he is doing as theft. After seeing the original and falling in love with the *Venus,* he refuses to create his picture by tracing or painting over another nude. Although the whores laugh at this, and Angelo tells him that he is only "painting the appearance of a picture" (*PF,* 87), Fidelman "paints as though he were painting the original . . . with what is left of his heart" (*PF,* 88).

This is the first story that shows Fidelman achieving a sense of artistic elevation that is based on one of his own creations. Because his copy is the best piece of work he has ever done, and because painting it has given him the feeling of having produced a work of art, he falls in love with it. A number of critics have interpreted Fidelman's reaction to his paintings as nothing more than self-love, "and it is selflessness that Fidelman—like Roy Hobbs, Frank Alpine, S. Levin and Yakov Bok before him—needs most to learn" (Ducharme, 137). His "stealing" of his own painting illustrates his inability to transcend the demands of self-love rather than his feeling that to steal the genuine Titian would be immoral. There is no inner growth here, just conceit: "The struggle of his characters 'against self,' Malamud declares, is 'basic'" (Siegel, 119).

This struggle continues in "A Pimp's Revenge," in which Fidelman attempts to exorcise his remembrances of his childhood with his mother and sister Bessie. He paints a masterpiece but has too little understanding both of art and his own life to leave it alone and in the end destroys it in an attempt to make it "perfect." The tale begins with Fidelman kicking "apart a trial canvas, copy of one he had been working on for years, his foot through the poor mother's mouth, destroyed the son's insipid puss, age about ten. It deserved death for not coming to life" (*PF,* 95). As in "Still Life" and "Naked Nude," his painting is constrained by his inability to cope with his past, art and life being seen as inextricably joined. As Malamud himself said: "It isn't life versus art necessarily; it's life *and* art. On Fidelman's tombstone read: 'I kept my finger in art'" (Field 1975, 13). At this stage, it is life that baffles him and prevents him, along with his lack of talent, from successfully pursuing art.

Obsessed with a photograph that Bessie has sent him of his mother and himself as a boy, Fidelman tries to create not only a painting based on the photo but also an idealized childhood that makes him better than he was or is. He invents a relationship between mother and son that, because of her death when Fidelman was six or seven years old, never existed. As his mistress, the prostitute Esmeralda, says to him: "To me it's as though you were trying to paint yourself into your mother's arms" (*PF*, 122). His guilt over not crying at his mother's funeral partly explains his being more relaxed when carving Madonnas; that is, when working on an image that is predetermined and does not require Fidelman to agonize over his mother's image. Of course it could be argued that his Madonnas are idealized images of his mother and that that is the reason they are so impressive. For Fidelman, though, it is in paint that he tries to express his artistic abilities, such as they are, and which requires that he come to grips with his past: "The truth is I am afraid to paint, like I might find out something about myself" (*PF*, 116). After five years' work, he cannot successfully complete his painting because he cannot create a sufficiently idealistic visage for his mother, nor can he paint himself with her in a relationship that never was. That there is a bit of Susskind in her shows that he is also still grappling with his Jewish past and is not at peace with it.

There are days when Fidelman "stood in terror before 'Mother and Son' and shivered with every stroke he put down" (*PF*, 131). He decides to cease trying to paint his mother and to try "Brother and Sister," thinking he can cope with Bessie better than he could with "Momma." He is, of course, still trying to come to grips with his past: "Indeed, Fidelman, turn his back as he will, always seems to resurrect Bessie and their dear, dead mother."[6] With Esmeralda serving as a model for Bessie, this painting fails also, and Esmeralda burns the photo, symbolically ending Fidelman's attempt to regain his mother through art, though he later bemoans her loss. He then paints what he calls "my most honest piece of work" (*PF*, 142), Esmeralda and himself as "Prostitute and Procurer." Leaving his own face in, he realizes that "I am what I became from a young age" (*PF*, 142). Though immediately trying to deny it, Fidelman does seem to have grasped an essential truth about himself: he is selfish, incapable of expressing true emotion. "Only when aesthetics become integrated with human emotions and Fidelman's physical and spiritual desires are no longer separate entities, can he begin his search for the perfection to which he aspires."[7]

The limitations of his character lead him to justify immoral behavior in the name of art, and Esmeralda returns to prostitution while Fidelman paints. He even thinks of giving Ludovico a percentage of the girl's earnings so that he can spend more time painting while the ex-pimp manages her. Art is related to prostitution. As she returns to her work,

Esmeralda is cynical: "'For art,' she said, then after a moment, bitterly, 'art, my ass'" (PF, 138). The price for a Madonna becomes the same as that for Esmeralda's services. In another instance of his moral bankruptcy, instead of having taken the trouble to learn the words of the Kaddish (the prayer for the dead), Fidelman has never bothered to say it for his mother, preferring to use art instead: "How do you paint a Kaddish?" (PF, 113) is his implied thought. Because of Fidelman's selfishness and self-consciousness, art and the artist become unethical; he uses people and religion only as a means to the end of artistic creation. As Robert Scholes observes: "Even the artist's name in this tale dwindles from Fidelman to F."[8]

His concern with producing a masterwork has removed Fidelman from real life. He is aware that when buying food "you get down to brass tacks" (PF, 102), but Esmeralda, having stayed with him because she thought an artist must know about life, discovers that he knows even less than she. Unlike Fidelman, Esmeralda would always choose life over art. To Fidelman's statement, "Without art there's no life to speak of, at least for me. If I'm not an artist, then I'm nothing," she replies, "Personally, I think you have a lot to learn" (PF, 124). Because of his ignorance of life, Fidelman can be neither a man nor an artist. His wish that he could guess what artistic movement will come next, his belief that everything has already been done, show his lack of understanding that movements come out of life and cannot be created in a vacuum. These problems will reach a climax in the next tale.

"Pictures of the Artist" is the most stylistically experimental of the stories. Robert Ducharme correctly considers it to be Fidelman's journey through both the underworld and his subconscious (Ducharme, 131), and Sheldon Grebstein calls it "a neo-Joycean, comitragic, surrealistic, stream-of-consciousness, visionary sequence, perhaps a burst of true madness in poor Fidelman but also containing a portion of almost coherent narrative which advances the story line. There is nothing remotely like it in Malamud's earlier writing" (Grebstein, 43).

In "Pictures of the Artist" Fidelman reaches the nadir of his experiences as a would-be artist. Traveling around Italy exhibiting holes in the ground as sculpture, he believes "that is Art which is made by the artist to be Art" (PF, 156) and "Form may be and often is the content of Art" (PF, 159). In his desperation to be an artist of some kind, he has convinced himself that the means (Form) are the end (Art). There is a further lessening of his compassion from the previous tale in his refusal to return the ten lire admission fee to the poor man who needs it to buy bread for his children. This poor man drowns himself and returns as a ghostly figure who is also the devil and has overtones of Susskind, with his black stockings and bowed legs. Completing the analogy between the holes and graves, the figure pushes Fidelman into one of them and refills it with earth. Fidelman has been digging his own grave because, as the figure tells him, "You have not yet learned what is the difference between something and nothing" (*PF*, 160). This applies to both his understanding of art and of human compassion.

The quality of compassion in the apparition is Susskind, whose main role in this tale is that of Jesus. In a sermon on the mount, he preaches mercy, then tells Fidelman not to try to paint him, as that is a sin; Fidelman must give up his paints and follow Susskind-Christ if he is to have a chance for salvation. Art has blinded him to his true needs. Although he drops his brushes into the Dead Sea, he saves one and uses it to paint Susskind so that "I will be remembered forever in human history" (*PF*, 164). Fidelman's concern is still with artistic fame and not with inner growth and compassion. While swearing to Susskind that he will now destroy all his artist's equipment, he later thinks how difficult it will be to hide his talent. He has yet to accept that he is talentless. This hallucination ends with Fidelman betraying Susskind and using his 39 pieces of silver to buy paints, brushes, and canvas. He watches Susskind's crucifixion from behind a mask, as though ashamed; however, Fidelman has not changed.

Susskind later reappears, still pressing Fidelman to choose compassion over art. This time Fidelman fantasizes a talking light bulb, in a scene that Philip Roth calls "Malamud the folk comic at his best. . . ."[9] He is still trying to leave his mark for the future, and Susskind is saying there are better ways than cave painting, but it is too late for Fidelman to learn. Susskind tries to get Fidelman to go "upstairs" to see his dying sister, but Fidelman considers his painting more important, taking the callous attitude that "it's no fault of mine if people die" (*PF*, 173). Since we are most likely in Fidelman's subconscious here, we learn what he truly thinks and feels. He hates the past, sees himself as a failure, and does not want to see Bessie "until my work here is done" (*PF*, 173); that is, until he is a success. "What is of major importance is that Fidelman's unconscious associations are not with fulfilled ability, but rather with loss, disappointment, frustration, impotence, and death, those very forces he has been evading in his conscious life . . ." (Alter 1981, 140).

A major change in his attitude does occur during this encounter, however, beginning with yet another ego-based reaction, that neither

Napoleon nor Van Gogh received advice from a bulb. Susskind understands Fidelman well enough to appeal to his sense of self in order to
move him toward a sense of pity and humanity. The cave in which he is
painting and talking with the bulb is located below Bessie's New Jersey
house, and her brother has been coming and going without seeing her,
even though she is always alone. Finally, he accepts Susskind's counsel
and criticism and goes upstairs to see her—a long way for Fidelman. This
act gives him the moral right to move toward a secular salvation in the
last tale. He accepts Susskind as his Virgil, who led Dante out of hell,
seeing him as the moral conscience from whom he must no longer run.
Like Frank Alpine, Fidelman has risen from a grave in which he was
earlier buried, to new ethical possibilities.

By the time we reach the final tale, "Glass Blower of Venice,"
Fidelman's personality has been stripped bare. Under the influence of
Beppo, a master glass blower and husband of Fidelman's mistress, he
slowly achieves a level of selflessness and compassion that he did not
possess before. He also finally learns to accept his limitations as an artist.
Fidelman notices that Beppo "looked in his handsome way much like his
mother" (*PF*, 195); in learning to love him, Fidelman may be trying to
create a relationship that he never had with his mother because of her
early death. Tony Tanner observes of Fidelman: "He becomes an 'assistant' and we recognize the term as honorific in Malamud's moral universe" (Tanner 1971, 339). It is not that Beppo is a mother surrogate; he
is a teacher of morality and compassion, like Morris Bober or Shmuel.

Fidelman describes to Beppo "the failures of his life in art" (*PF*, 192).
Beppo must destroy the remaining works to free Fidelman from their
tyranny, from his belief that he may still be capable of producing art.
Indeed, even after Beppo has begun teaching him about the craft of glass
blowing, Fidelman still attempts to transmute the craft into art. Beppo
shouts at him, "A fanatic never knows when to stop. It's obvious you
want to repeat your fate" (*PF*, 205) and "half a talent is worse than none"
(*PF*, 206). Fidelman does learn, however, as can be seen by the fact that
he seems finally to accept that he will never be a great artist. More
important, he loses his self-centeredness, saying "I love you" for the first
time in his life. He finds that "he watched the glass blower and foresaw
his needs, in essence a new experience for him" (*PF*, 203). His assistantship is in love as well as in craft. Fidelman's thinking that "you worked
and loved at once" (*PF*, 202) shows that he has, through Beppo, learned
to combine "the aesthetic and the physical, the spirit and the flesh . . ."
(Rubin, 22).

Malamud is saying that becoming selfless through loving another teaches things in addition to love. Fidelman is able to put his grandiose hopes of becoming a great artist behind him largely because love has taught him the true value of things. He need no longer base his judgment of himself as a man on whether or not he is successful in art—a great advance from his attitude in "A Pimp's Revenge." Because of love, Fidelman can return to America to preserve Beppo's family, an act of selflessness he could not have made in any of the earlier tales.

At the end of the story he blows a beautiful bowl, which is then stolen, presumably by an admirer. Fidelman is left with his love of Beppo and the knowledge that he was able to produce something that had the qualities of art. He will not become obsessed by this again, as we are told that "in America he worked as a craftsman in glass and loved men and women" (*PF*, 208). It is the loving that is important. Beppo, like Susskind before him, tried to teach Fidelman that selflessness and compassion are more important than bad art.

Malamud opened *Pictures of Fidelman* with an epigraph from Yeats: "The intellect of man is forced to chose / Perfection of the life, or of the work. . . ." Fidelman says that he wants both. What his adventures prove is that Yeats was correct. Malamud's attitude in the novel is that "perfection of the life" is more important than the work. Personally, Malamud may have had a soft spot for Fidelman's original desire, as he reputedly told an interviewer, "I want my books to contain a feeling for humanity and to be a work of art."[10] He will explore this problem further in his next novel, *The Tenants,* in which the protagonist, Harry Lesser, shares Fidelman's obsession with creating perfection in art, in this case in the form of the novel. Like Fidelman, Lesser avoids humanity, is short on human compassion, and has no understanding of love. Unlike him, Lesser never learns the lessons that Susskind and Beppo taught Fidelman.

Chapter Seven
The Tenants

Blacks and Whites

When Malamud was asked why he wrote *The Tenants,* he answered, "Jews and blacks, the period of the troubles in New York City, the teachers strike, the rise of black activism, the mix-up of cause and effect. I thought I'd say a word" (Stern, 61). As *A New Life* discussed aspects of McCarthyism and *The Fixer* focused on a particular period in the history of Tsarist Russia, so *The Tenants* treats issue of black anti-Jewish sentiment in the 1960s, despite the long and vigorous Jewish support given to black groups and causes.

Before the novel's appearance, Malamud had published two short stories treating relationships between blacks and Jews: "Angel Levine" (1955) and "Black Is My Favorite Color" (1963). The earlier tale focuses on the Job-like suffering of the protagonist, Manishevitz, and the question of whether his faith can extend to belief in a black, Jewish angel who claims to be a messenger from God. Relief from suffering for Manishevitz and full angelhood for Levine depends on the protagonist's ability to extend his idea of Jewishness to all human beings, and Levine's color makes the task much more difficult. Manishevitz's success leads to spiritual redemption for both, a much more optimistic ending than the more likely one of *The Tenants.*

"Black Is My Favorite Color" relies on realism rather than fantasy in its first-person, pessimistic rendition of the futility of offering love in a poisoned racial climate. The subtlety of prejudice is such that even a blind black man can detect a white person. Ultimately, Nat Lime cannot overcome the superior position that he, as a white man, holds in society; the black world is closed to him, and each race is going in a different direction.

In *The Tenants,* Harry Lesser and Willie Spearment reflect each other's prejudices. Even before Willie arrives on the scene, Harry's nightmares contain a black thug that he meets on the stairs. He wonders what it would be like to sleep with a black girl, and Willie's nervousness before asking him to read his manuscript causes Harry to muse: "Has he been seeing old Stepin Fetchit films . . . ?"[1] Malamud presents Willie at times as a stereotypical black man, one who responds easily to music and actually says: "Don't nobody have to tell me about rhythm" (*TT*, 87). Harry's reaction to the white, Jewish Irene being Willie's "sweet bitch" is laden with jealousy, not least because a black man is sleeping with her. When Harry and Irene sleep together, he denies it but Irene is aware of the racial implications: " . . . I have this awful feeling as though you and I are a couple of Charlies giving a nigger a boot in the ass" (*TT*, 148).

Perhaps even more than Harry, who tries early on to compensate for his prejudice by helping Willie with his writing, Willie is full of bigotry, as he is both antiwhite and anti-Jewish. Upon first meeting Harry, Willie refuses to shake his hand. His loss of Irene to Harry hurts Willie's pride, but it is doubtful that he loves her. She is more of a status symbol to him than anything else, because Willie refers to her when first introducing her to Harry as "his white chick, not giving her name" (*TT*, 42). As the prestige of a black man having a white woman wanes politically, so Willie begins to end his relationship with Irene, refusing to hold her hand in public or to take her to Harlem.

The "half-dozens" bring out both characters' latent racism: Harry calls Willie a "filthy nigger prick" because "I know you want to hear it" (*TT*, 134), and Willie calls Harry a "Kike apeshit thieven Jew" (TT, 134). Each character is aware of what words will most hurt the other's racial or ethnic pride, and this reaches its peak in Willie's violent anti-Semitic stories which equate all that he hates in whites with the Jews. "The way to black freedom is against them," he says (*TT*, 220). The ending that this will lead to unless love or compassion intervenes is Willie's epithet, "Bloodsuckin Jew Niggerhater," followed by Harry's "Anti-Semitic Ape" (*TT*, 229).

There is some sense of hope implied by Malamud's references to smells. Upon first meeting Willie, Harry detects a "sulphurous smell . . ." (*TT*, 29–30) arising from his manuscript. This hellish aroma, which parallels Harry's negative attitude toward blacks, persists when he later begins to read Willie's stories. However, when he rereads the stories, the suffering, rage, and, possibly, tears that went into the writing cause him to detect "no smell at all" (*TT*, 66). Through being able to see Willie as a suffering human being, Harry's original prejudices disappear. When hatred later returns, so does the smell. While blacks and whites can detect a unique odor in the other—shades of the blind man in "Black Is My Favorite Color"—this aroma disappears when each is perceived by the other as human and not as black or white. Also, when truth, suffering, or compassion is perceived in the writing of each, an odor, or bigotry, disappears.

Willie's central concern in his own writing is to express the sufferings of blacks at the hands of whites. He feels that whites are incapable of understanding black experience or black feelings, and so cannot tell blacks anything of use about themselves. Indeed, he feels it is offensive when whites presume to try to write about blacks. Harry's attitude is that of an artist, a believer in the universality of which art is capable. He tells Willie, "If you're an artist you can't be a nigger . . ." (*TT*, 51) and "if the experience is about being human and moves me then you've made it my experience" (*TT*, 75). His stress is on the importance of form, which Willie resists as being part of white, not black, writing. Malamud was very much aware of the existence of this attitude: "'I expected trouble, but I didn't get it,' [he said] although some black writers complained that Malamud had no business portraying a violent black character's search for identity" (Suplee, F8). It should be noted that "Willie's own thoughts are rarely presented in the novel. Malamud seems to be sensitive to precisely that opprobrium which accrues to a white man who purports to be in Willie's words, 'an expert of black experience.'"[2]

Willie and Harry frequently see aspects of themselves in each other. Both are struggling as writers to put into order on paper elements of their experiences either that they do not fully understand—love, for Harry—or that require purgation so that they can live with themselves—the black situation in America for Willie. Harry lacks Willie's orientation to life, to real experience; Willie needs more of Harry's understanding of form, as when Harry tells him, "You can't turn black experience into literature just be writing it down" (*TT*, 74). Each writer becomes the other's victim because neither is capable of a sufficient depth of sympathy for the struggles and limitations of the other. Despite virtually taking on each other's persona—Willie becoming the obsessive writer and Harry sleeping with Irene—their relationship comes to revolve around selfishness: what use each can make of the other. Willie uses Harry for instruction in the writer's craft; Harry comes to rely on Willie to provide elements of life outside writing: women, parties, social consciousness. Their prejudices and lack of compassion will lead, most likely, to mutual destruction.

Art and Life

As in *Picture's of Fidelman*, there is a symbiotic relationship expressed in *The Tenants* between art and reality. In thinking about his difficulties in completing his novel, entitled *The Promised End*, Harry muses: "It was as though the book had asked him to say more than he knew . . ." (*TT*, 106). He hopes that writing it will teach him about love, something he admits to knowing little about. He cannot complete it because it is about love, and he must bring knowledge of the subject to the book rather than hoping that his protagonist can provide this understanding for him. Lesser, his name having symbolic importance because of his inability to love, neglects his aged father and Irene, much as Fidelman ignored his sister Bessie and never said Kaddish for his dead mother. Both protagonists hope that if they can complete their work of art they will complete themselves. Since for Malamud, "love—the total union with another person—is the primary means toward redemption and salvation" (Rubin, 22), Harry's ability or inability to achieve a loving relationship is crucially important to both his life and his writing.

Lesser is related in *The Tenants* to the painter Lazar Kohn. The model for Kohn's "abstract and fragmented 'Woman'" (*TT*, 109) was Kohn's mistress, just as Irene is Lesser's mistress. Kohn never was able to finish the painting (a success nonetheless), just as Lesser is unable to complete his novel—about his protagonist, Lazar Cohen. Given the nature of the art form, however, Lesser's novel will be a failure unless it is completed. Irene also possesses traits that directly relate her to Kohn's 'Woman,' who is described as "trying to complete herself through her own will, as willed by the painter. Otherwise she was an appearance of a face and body trying to make it through a forest of binding brush strokes" (*TT*, 110). Irene's attempts to complete herself, partly through psychoanalysis, have given way to the will of others—Willie and Harry. Her attempts to act on her own have been hampered by a lack of confidence and what appears to be a set of values based on the upbringing of a nice, Jewish girl, placing marriage and family first. She rebelled by becoming an actress and a mistress to a black man (though she had wanted to marry Willie), but she returns to conventionality in taking up with Harry, a white, Jewish writer. In the end she says, "I'm not career-oriented; I'd rather be married and have a family. . . . What a bourgeois shit I've become" (*TT*, 188). When she leaves Harry to go to San Fransisco alone, she breaks out of the "binding brush strokes," the wills of her art-obsessed lovers that have imprisoned her, and leaves the two writers to their own self-imposed prisons.

As Willie and Harry are both involved with Irene, so are they involved with the landlord Irving Levenspiel. Like Irene, the landlord serves as a touchstone for the writers' attitudes. To Willie, Levenspiel is never more than an exploiting landlord, a stereotype in much the same vein as Levenspiel's view of Willie as a "nigger." In relation to Harry, however, Levenspiel illustrates further his divorce from reality and compassion, because of art. Like Manishevitz, protagonist of "Angel Levine," Levenspiel has experienced an inundation of woes, which he relates to Harry no doubt in part to get him to move out through moving him emotionally. Nonetheless, that Harry can resist his pleas, in the name of art, only further reveals his own limitations: "But Lesser ignores Levenspiel's Job-like plight, just as Fidelman ignored Susskind. And Lesser ignores Levenspiel for the same ironic reason: to make a significant statement about humanity" (Cohen, 108). Harry tells him, "Something essential is missing that it takes time to find" (TT, 21). What is missing from his book is sympathy, mercy, and love, and his talking to the landlord about the pressures of form only justify Levenspiel's comment, "What's a make-believe novel, Lesser, against all my woes and miseries that I have explained to you?" (TT, 21). In "A Pimp's Revenge," Esmeralda shouts at Fidelman as she returns to prostitution to support his painting, "Art my ass" (TT, 138). Levenspiel echoes this bitter remark when he says, "Art my ass, in this world it's heart that counts" (TT, 22). Later, at the end of his rope, the desperate landlord tells Harry that he has "steady biting pains around my heart" (TT, 193). Harry does not feel these pains and sees some of the limitations he has imposed upon himself: "So much I no longer see or feel except in language. Life once removed" (TT, 107). It should be noted that the landlord's name is close to the Yiddish *Lebin shpiel,* playing life, something from which Harry keeps his distance.

Malamud's description of the writers finding out that their craft has taken over their lives and feelings is most effective: "Whereas Willie tries to create art out of life, Lesser tries to discover life through his art. Neither is successful" (Mesher, 62). Willie gives up Irene to concentrate on his book. When Irene tells Harry that her relationship with Willie is fading, Harry's excitement takes an odd turn: "He feels in himself a flow of language, a surge of words toward an epiphany. . . . He rises craving to write" (TT, 119–20). When Harry feels what he thinks is love for Irene, he worries that it "might complicate his life and slow down his work, it did not. . . . But mostly what happened was that he was often high on reverie and felt renewed energy for work" (*TT*, 150). Having an emotion attached to real life instead of to words alone makes him feel free, and optimistic, and his writing improves. His reaction disproves his earlier idea that he might learn about love only through writing. Unfortunately, because of his rigidity and egotism, he cannot put real love first, cannot put into practice his realization that "I've got to write but I've got to more than write" (*TT*, 140).

This obsession with writing instead of real life eventually takes over Willie too, who finds himself moving from a comparatively easygoing approach to writing to one where he resists going to Harry's party because he wants to stay with his work. As he becomes more absorbed in words, Harry's influence is such that he tells him: "The worst about it is I don't want to do anything else but sit there and write. It's getting me scared" (*TT*, 87). Part of the reason for Willie's being so easily drawn into Harry's orbit lies in the fact that like Harry, Willie is in the process of creating himself through his book, taking the tragedies of black powerlessness in America and transforming them. It is as though if he can, through fiction and later through imagined action, turn blacks into chosen people, history will be nullified and Willie will gain stature as a human being. Willie dislikes Harry's insistence on form because he sees it as the white man's way. Unfortunately, Willie cannot create literature through an avoidance of form, through a reliance on anarchy and emotions as the opposite to "white" order and the mind. Above all, Willie wants power for his people and himself, and he hopes to create action through his words. His pseudonym, Bill Spear, combines overtones of literature, violence, and the physical (the phallic), in contrast to Harry Lesser's name, which exudes self-control and passionlessness. Through his new name, Willie wishes to obliterate his past and become a new person. David Mesher observes that "Willie, in many ways, is a 'nigger': the stereotyped ghetto black. Bill, the devoted artist, is not. . . . Willie, unable to be Bill, reverts to the stereotype of the ghetto black . . ." (Mesher, 67).

The issue of self-creation is highlighted in the "autobiographical" sections of Willie's book. Harry assumes that the first 148 pages are autobiography; the favored of three titles is *Missing Life*. Willie tells him, and Irene confirms it, that this apparently realistic part is made up, whereas four of the five stories that follow are true but not about Willie himself, though there are parallels (Harlem, prison) with his own life. Irene says that "he changes his birthplace every time he talks about it. I

think he hates to remember it" (*TT*, 116). Since Willie cannot write with
any objectivity, one can assume that though it is not autobiography,
Missing Life contains much that has its roots in Willie's attempting to
come to terms with his own deprived past.

In trying to imbue his character Herbert Smith's experiences with a
"revolutionary mentality," Harry believes (and he seems likely to be
correct) that Willie "was attempting in his fiction to shed an incubus—
his former life. This was not necessarily bad in itself but could be bad if
he insisted, and he was insisting. As a result nobody in this long section
came halfway to life" (*TT*, 162).

Willie's writing fails because he cannot distance himself sufficiently
from feeling passionately about black struggle and oppression; he does
not understand the uses of form. Harry's writing fails because he is
bogged down in form and is too distant from real life. A subtle balance
must exist for the creation of successful art. Ultimately Willie uses his
writing for the purpose of purgation, confession, and politics, which
guarantees his failure. He realizes this and decides to give up writing,
despite Harry's remark that "art is action"; his rejoinder: "Action is my
action" (*TT*, 166).

Form and Content

In *The Tenants* there is a continuation of the prison motif that occurs in
various guises in all of Malamud's novels. Characters have been trapped
by their pasts, goals, mistakes, or personality flaws. In some instances a
literal structure has symbolized this entrapment, such as the store in *The
Assistant,* the cell in *The Fixer,* and the tenement in *The Tenants.* The
tenement in which Harry and Willie entomb themselves effectively
blocks out much of the real world. When the world does enter demanding concern and compassion, as with a whimpering dog with a bleeding
eye, Harry immediately removes it from the building, ignoring sounds of
"muted cries, distant wailing . . ." (*TT*, 24) that seem to float in from
the city outside. Harry resists Levenspiel's pleas and will not even open
his door to him; Willie simply hides or flees. The isolation of Harry and
Willie in the tenement permits Malamud to focus on them in great
detail. There is also a symbolic parallel between the disintegrating
building and the state of race relations in the United States. The building
may be seen to verge on becoming an objective correlative for the
emotions roused by the claustrophobic nature of the protagonists' obses-

sions with writing and the junglelike ferocity of their eventual confrontations, in which racial issues are central.

The Tenants is an essentially gloomy and pessimistic novel, not possessing even the limited and qualified optimism that exists at the end of *The Fixer*. Given what has happened in the story, the likelihood of the interracial wedding taking place in the future between Harry and Mary and Willie and Irene is remote. The tone and tenor of the characterizations and plot stress hopelessness, and the violence that erupts is not at all surprising. With the possible exception of Irene, none of the characters is particularly amenable to sympathy from the reader. Cynthia Ozick thinks the characterizations are flawed, but not completely so: "The balance was unequal, the protagonists unfairly matched, the Jew too hesitant and disciplined, the black too spontaneous and unschooled."[3] She wonders why Malamud did not present an Ellison rather than an Eldridge Cleaver and concludes that it was for the purpose of "novelistic bite and drama. . . ." However, Harry eventually realizes that Willie is both a "goy" and "a ferocious, a mythic, anti-Semite" (Ozick, 92). She sees Malamud as reflecting the times, stating that he "did not make Willie. He borrowed him—he mimicked him—from the literature and the politics of the black movement. Willie is the black dream that is current in our world. Blacks made him. Few blacks disavow him" (Ozick, 95).

Writing in 1967, Leslie Fiedler observes that Jews are the only white Americans who might feel no guilt toward blacks since they neither owned slaves nor had any part in lynchings. Moreover Jews can see in blacks a people who are treated as they themselves once were, a people who in America have taken on the role of pariah that, but for them, Jews might have. Yet largely because of the Jews' former roles as landlords, shopkeepers, teachers, and social workers in the black ghettos, "just as society must have a scapegoat, so hatred must have a symbol. Georgia has the Negro. Harlem has the Jew."[4] Both Ozick and Fiedler view a character like Willie in terms of the extremes of the times. As the novel is set in the midst of these extremes, Malamud's characterization of Willie is appropriate. Harry's attempts to cope with his own subtle prejudices and his feelings of guilt because of them, his positive feelings toward a fellow writer, and the flaws that exist in his own personality and character combine to create the tension that comes out when he confronts & Willie.

While the novel mixes reality and fantasy, the reader perceives "all action filtered through Lesser's fanciful thoughts and nightmares. Wil-

lie's internalizings remain shrouded" (Siegel, 138). Blending fantasy
with reality is not a new technique for Malamud, as its use can be seen in
The Natural, in *The Fixer*, in "Pictures of the Artist" in *Pictures of
Fidelman*, and in a number of his short stories. Fantasy in *The Tenants*
includes Harry's turning the building into a jungle located in the middle
of Manhattan—an island on an island: " . . . this sceptered isle on a
silver sea, this Thirty-first Street and Third Avenue. This forsaken
house" (*TT*, 5). Willie's arrival adds an allusion to Daniel Defoe, with
Harry as Robinson Crusoe and Willie as a frustrated Friday full of rage.

This use of fantasy takes the reader into Harry's subconscious. We
learn of his fears and hopes through his reveries, visions, and dreams. One
critic sees Malamud's use of these states of mind as expressing "the
inevitable interrelationships of characters, . . . where they record the
progressive and tragic interlocking of Harry and Willie's destinies."[5]
The interlocking of destinies can be seen in Harry's dream of Willie's
poem concerning Willie's sex life with Irene, followed by Willie eating
a large bone that may be Harry's leg. This nightmare occurs while Harry
is in bed with Irene, when Willie has not yet been told of their
relationship. The ending containing descriptions of the interracial marriages also illustrates an aspect of the two writers' relationship, in this
instance leading to a positive, highly optimistic, conclusion. There are
numerous examples of this use of reverie and dreams as a plot device.

Malamud presents mirrors within mirrors in what the reader must
decipher to cope with the plot: "Often, the reader will follow along in an
event in Lesser's life, only to learn that the event is in Lesser's fiction. The
reader is irritated, but he knows how Lesser feels: the boundaries of art
and life are not so easily determined" (Helterman 1985, 90–91). Malamud uses Willie's writing the same way, blurring the distinction between fiction and reality. The cumulative effect of this is that the reader
frequently must decide which book he is reading: "The one Malamud has
written? The one each of us reads? The one that the character called
Lesser is writing? Or the one that the nameless writer, in the novel that
Lesser is writing, is also trying to write?" (Hassan 1977, 56). The reader
is forced into the writers' dilemma of the overlapping nature of art and
life. Interestingly it is the art, the artificial, that is frequently more
gripping than reality, largely because of Malamud's skill in presenting
the obduracy and fanaticism with which both writers, lacking a full
understanding of reality, attempt to transmute partially understood
feelings into fiction. As in "A Pimp's Revenge," Malamud explores the
anguish of a creator who is incapable of completing his most important

creation, perhaps only in part because the unfinished masterpiece is "the only existence that the artist has. Lesser feels that he has only one masterpiece in him, and at the moment he finishes *The Promised End,* he will cease to be an artist" (Helterman 1985, 91). Willie's destruction of Harry's manuscript is tantamount to murder, in that he prevents him from discovering those aspects of himself—love in particular—that would make him a complete human being. However, because Harry is unlikely to learn what he must from his writing, the destruction is a mercy killing, a piece of dramatic irony, in that it has freed Harry from a quest that he would never complete.

Malamud "thinks of *The Tenants* as a sort of Prophetic warning against fanaticism. 'The book,' he says, 'argues for the invention of choices to outwit tragedy.'"[6] When asked why he needed three endings, Malamud replied, "Because one wouldn't do" (Stern, 61). It could be argued, in fact, that two more endings precede the three. The first is a reverie wherein Harry imagines Levenspiel setting fire to the building, thus providing an end both to himself and his novel. There may be implied here some sense of guilt on Harry's part for his deafness to Levenspiel's pleas, but if there is guilt, it does not affect his actions. A second possible ending occurs when Willie burns Harry's manuscript, which has been ten years in the writing.

The three major endings take place in the final 24 pages of the novel and reflect the possible outcomes of black-white relations in America. The first is apparently hopeful: black and white/Jew will intermarry and solve the problem of racial conflict. However, there are many caveats and hesitancies expressed. The chief says: "When our black daughter marry the white mens we do not rejoice . . ." (*TT,* 210). Shortly afterward he adds: "The ceremony of reconciliation is useless. Men say the words of peace but they do not forgive the other" (*TT,* 211–12). The rabbi is nervous and "stares in amazement at the assemblage" (*TT,* 209), later saying: "My rabbinical colleagues will criticize me strongly for performing this ceremony . . ." (*TT,* 216). Harry and Irene's fathers clearly disapprove, and David Belinsky "smiles striken" (*TT,* 214). Harry imagines this ending "like an act of love, the end of my book, if I dared." Irene's response within the fantasy is "You're not so smart . . ." (*TT,* 217).

The second ending concludes a period in which Harry has destroyed Willie's typewriter, having found that his own paper gave off an unpleasant odor, that of hate. He has had a reverie of being destroyed in another fire, this time set by Willie. He now no longer writes; that is, he no longer attempts to find out about love. The building has become a jungle and each strikes the other in the place where his own group is most prone to being stereotyped, thus showing how much like the other each has become. So, Harry sinks an ax in Willie's brain, and Willie cuts off Harry's balls. Like the previous ending, this one is fantasy; it does not occur. The only hope is seen in the final phrase: "Each, thought the writer, feels the anguish of the other" (*TT*, 230). Of course, it is too late for this feeling to have an effect.

The final ending of the novel is Levenspiel's cry for mercy. Since the first ending is unlikely, the only way to avoid the second may be through Levenspiel's plea that black and white have mercy for each other as struggling fellow human beings. While some critics think this triple ending is inadequate, actually an avoidance of an ending, Malamud's provision of choice here mirrors reality. He admitted in an interview four years after the novel's publication: "It's impossible to predict—it may go one way; it may go another" (Field 1975, 14). As Saul Bellow's Dean Corde points out in *The Dean's December* (1982), the black underclass is growing and whites may well have given up on attempts to integrate its members into society: "Those that can be advanced into the middle class, let them be advanced. The rest? Well, we do our best by them. We don't have to do any more. They kill some of us. Mostly they kill themselves . . . ."[7] Not much room for mercy here.

Chapter Eight
Dubin's Lives

Lives: Real and Imagined

Malamud stated in an interview that *"Dubin's Lives* was his attempt at bigness, at summing up what he had learned over the long haul. 'I was already approaching 60 when I began it and I had to be very severe with myself,' he said. 'What had my experience totaled up to? What did I know up to this point?'"[1] Malamud implies that *Dubin's Lives* is related to and extends his previous concerns. Although William Dubin is Jewish and there are some Jewish references, Jewishness is not an important factor in the novel. However, there is a continuity of theme and characterization, particularly in the need of the protagonist to move from self-containment to an expansion of the heart that encompasses the needs of others. As with Harry Lesser in *The Tenants,* Dubin only partially achieves this, although he does develop further than Lesser.

Dubin is a biographer who believes that he can learn about life through reading the lives of others and writing biographies himself. Early in the novel he shows that he is aware of the problematic nature of this belief, that "a good writer adventures beyond the uses of language, or what's there to put into words? Yet the truth is some do not: of them Dubin is one."[2] He feels that there is an underlying similarity in life's stages, that by reading and writing about the lives of others one can learn "where life goes" (*DL,* 12). His approach is reductive in that the pattern he perceives in the lives of others convinces him that he is learning more about living through his vicarious experiences than he would were he doing the living himself. Also, if life consists of repeating patterns ("joys, celebrations, crises, illusions, losses, sorrows" [*DL,* 12]) the implication is that unpredictability is not recognized, and life becomes something one can organize, essentially antilife.

Because of Dubin's belief that writing is living, "he is languishing within from unending introspection. . . ."[3] He recognizes that "those who write about life reflect about life" (*DL,* 130) and believes that this reflection provides the best way of understanding existence, "would make the difference between badly and decently knowing" (*DL,* 326), and would teach him what others understand better than he. However, actual life continually startles him out of his languor, lending doubt to the efficacy of biography as a teacher. He suffers from his division of art and life, similar to the way Harry Lesser does.

Sigmund Freud would not support Dubin's stance: "Freud devastated Dubin: 'Anyone turning biographer has committed himself to lies, to concealment, to hypocracy, to flattery, and even to hiding his own lack of understanding: for biographical truth is not to be had, and even if it were it couldn't be useful'" (*DL,* 299). The truth of this observation can be seen in the fact that "Dubin is the bearer of no superior moral insight; nor is his behavior especially admirable. . . ."[4] This is so despite the fact that he spends most of his time reflecting about life and lives and considering the moral implications of the lives of others and his own.

It is in his relationship to his family, friends, and mistress that the dichotomy between biography and life can most clearly be seen. Toward the end of the novel, Dubin's wife accuses him of not being a loving man and Dubin agrees, adding that he is grateful to Kitty for showing him his flaws so that he might be a better biographer. Angered, Kitty replies, "Everything sooner or later goes back to your biographies. That's your grand passion—if you could fuck your books you'd have it made" (*DL,* 337). Even morality is divorced from human engagement, as Dubin wonders whether "his deceit to Kitty might induce dishonesty in his work" (*DL,* 238).

Dubin assumes that his "lacking nature" cannot be changed, that he is what he is. Development as a human being takes second place—if it has a place at all—to develop as a biographer, to applying life's lessons to an abstract understanding of the lives of others, on paper. He wonders whether the biographer's life, far from having thrust him into the human existence, has curbed and moderated his character, "my nature subdued by how I've lived and the lives I've written . . ." (*DL,* 127). Though saddened by this, he accepts it, telling his daughter that someone remarked that "no valuable work is accomplished except at the expense of a life" (*DL,* 167).

This conclusion is not necessarily accurate. Leon Edel, Pulitzer Prize–winning biographer of Henry James, believes that "the committed biographer . . . writing with a sense of art and vocation, is at once more extrovert, more in touch with people and life, less obsessed than a narcissist like Dubin. A professional biographer embraces his way of expression through human sympathy and the gift of empathy. . . ."[5]

Although he also states that Dubin is certainly no hack, Dubin clearly lacks many of the qualities that Edel feels a professional biographer requires. He does not perceive his work as detached from himself but hopes, like Harry Lesser, to learn about himself through it and, his ability to feel sympathy or empathy for his subjects, for Lawrence in particular, is very limited. His main problem, however, is that he lacks sufficient self-knowledge: "The most successful modern biographers have been those who knew themselves before they embarked upon the knowing of others" (Edel, 63).

Dubin does have a certain amount of self-understanding; however, he tries to impose upon his limited, reflective self ideas from the literature and the lives he has read. Often, these ideas do not fit Dubin. He tells Fanny, somewhat sententiously, that "what the poets say about seizing the day . . . is incredibly true. If you don't live life to the hilt, or haven't, for whatever reason, you will regret it . . ." (*DL*, 34). When he adds that by living life he means largely through books, Fanny responds: "And that gives you your big charge? To me life is what you do. I want it to enjoy, and not make any kind of moral lesson or fairy tale out of it" (*DL*, 35).

The upshot of this difference in attitude comes when Fanny offers herself to Dubin, who rejects her: "Her face reddened. She was angered. 'All this beautiful bullshit about seize the day and what life is all about. . . .' Dubin reached for his pen and after a while slowly began to write" (*DL*, 38). While he would like to be able to live an active life, it is the process of ordering life through writing that most appeals to him. He can turn from Fanny to pen and paper because he appreciates the control over life that writing gives him. Later, after their abortive trip to Venice, Dubin castigates himself for "allowing desire to overflow the workaday life. . . . He must rid himself of his ongoing half-jealous thoughts of the girl—these irritating intrusive two-bit emotions—make the flood-waters of the unconscious recede. He had once more to be the man he'd been; *who Dubin was*" (*DL*, 122).

His obsession with order and with avoiding the "floodwaters of the unconscious" shows how unsuitable Dubin is to be the biographer of the life of D. H. Lawrence. He has already published a biography of Thoreau, another writer with whom he seems to have little in common. While these choices may appear to illustrate Dubin's ability to move away from a concern with self, both writers have qualities that he would very much like to possess. Thoreau's insight into nature, his love affair with it, was something Dubin wished to grasp. Mirrors within mirrors, Malamud himself used Thoreau, through Dubin, to engage with nature: "I had Dubin in the country . . . and I was eager to handle nature seriously. In familiarizing myself with the writings of Thoreau I had the opportunity to reflect about nature" (Tyler, 32). For Dubin, writing Thoreau's life served as an attempt to complete a part of himself, and he admits that while working on the biography he had "for a time become the celebate nature lover, or so it had seemed" (*DL,* 23). Dubin moves very much away from this stance when he decides to immerse himself in the life of D. H. Lawrence, again attempting to complete an uncompleted part of himself.

Lawrence's ideas and theories are central to Dubin's development. Despite important differences between Lawrence's view of life and Thoreau's, Dubin finds in both a stress on the importance of living life to the full, of seizing the day, something which he is incapable of doing. Both men are father figures to him, the theme of fathers and sons being a common one in Malamud's fiction. Edel perceives another possible reason for the attraction of these two writers for Dubin: "I would suggest that Thoreau seems right for Dubin as a fellow narcissist, and Walden Pond had a splendid mirror-like surface for them both. Lawrence is partly right because of his sexual narcissism" (Edel, 63).

Given the intertwining of Dubin's life with the subjects of his biographies, it is not surprising to discover that, about Lawrence, he thinks "there's something he wants me to know" (*DL,* 171). Dubin lacks passion and is suspicious of it; he fears the instinctual, prefers the known. Even on his daily walk-run he rarely ventures off the road he knows, and he berates himself for not being more adventurous. When he does accidentally lose sight of the road in a snowstorm and wanders into unknown territory, he almost perishes. It is notable that he is saved by Kitty, who here symbolizes the safety of convention, of the known. He feels that he ought to change his life before it changes him in ways he does not want. That is why, despite his recognition of the great personality difference between Lawrence and himself, a difference that Fanny, Evan Ondyk, and Maud openly express awareness of, Dubin feels he must try to understand the ideas of the great writer. Although he resists it, he would nonetheless like to bring into his life the physical, instinctual aspects that have been subsumed by the intellectual. (Even as a child, Dubin admired control, writing "'Will i am.'" [*DL,* 175]) For Lawrence, this suppression of the passions, of love and instinct by the intellect or "spirit" is a great sin that leads to the development of incomplete people.

Dubin flagellates himself with a vision of a hypercritical, anti-Semitic Lawrence: "Work which should be an extension of human consciousness you distort to the end-all of existence. You write muckspout lives because you fear you have no life to live. Your impotence is Jewish self-hatred. I detest and loathe you! . . . *Tha s'lltna touch me*" (*DL,* 319).

Dubin is only nominally Jewish, but Malamud includes several minor references to Jews in the novel, particularly by siting a synagogue within view from Fanny's bedroom window. Occasionally Dubin prays: "It was a way of addressing the self; God has a tin ear" (*DL,* 219). Because he has made a religion of biography, he can only delve into himself, another life like those about which he writes and reads; he is not concerned with eternal questions. Ironically, Kitty relates a dream she had in which she saw Dubin as a rabbi. When she talks to him about their marriage, which she sees as having failed, the implication is that, had Dubin possessed more religious—spiritual—qualities, the situation might have been different. Dubin, however, has other areas that he would like to develop—more physical, Lawrencean ones.

Although Jewishness is a minor factor in the novel, one critic sees Dubin as having internalized certain stereotypical Jewish traits that support Lawrence's imaginary accusations against him: "But there is a Jewish quality that persists. For better or worse Jewishness is defined by Dubin as a sense of obligation, a way of doing things characterized by the restraint of decency."[6] I am not convinced that Dubin's sense of obligation is at all related to his definition of Jewishness, nor that his restraint is particularly related to decency. Elsewhere, Daniel Fuchs refers to him as a "blob, a deracinated, self-cancelling neuter, who is barely Jew or pagan" (Fuchs, 211); this describes him more accurately. It is Kitty, not Dubin, who decides to raise Maud as Jewish "out of respect for her father . . ." (*DL,* 106). Maud's father does not appear to care one way or the other, his sense of obligation and restraint coming from other sources.

Dubin's affair with Fanny Bick helps him understand Lawrence better, just as Lawrence helps him understand his feelings for Fanny. He wonders whether his being steeped in Lawrencean theories of sexuality has changed his usual way of responding to eroticism. At one point his basic predilection momentarily reappears: " 'Control yourself,' he warned himself, and didn't like the sound of it" (*DL,* 274). Although he does not fully agree with Lawrence's ideas, he still finds that a part of himself, an undeveloped part, has been enriched. He perceives this enrichment in

Lawrencean terms: "With this girl I know the flowering pleasure, heathen innocence, of the natural life" (*DL,* 219). Dubin being Dubin, he must put this to practical use, a most un-Lawrencean thing to do. After lovemaking, he muses on his biography in progress, thinking that his affair with Fanny "couldn't have come at a better moment. He understood Lawrence more fully, his religion of sexuality: a belief in the blood, the flesh, as wiser than the intellect" (*DL,* 219). He also notes that his "visits to Fanny sparked his work. Ideas swarmed in Dubin's mind" (*DL,* 232). This is reminiscent of Harry Lesser's reaction to his affair with Irene. Like Dubin, Lesser also finds that his woman sparks his work. Neither writer can respond to his relationship as an end in itself.

Some critics think that what Dubin suffers from is nothing more than a midlife crisis. Malamud denied this, saying that "the novel was not about middle age . . . but about a man's crisis during a period of three years. I am writing about one human being, not all human beings" (Tyler, 32). While Dubin has some problems that are unique to himself, largely his obsession to live through biographies, he does share others with the rest of humanity: he has a middle-aged concern with death and has chosen both Thoreau and Lawrence, at least in part, because he recognizes that "as writers their themes were alike—death and resurrection" (*DL,* 32). He sees Fanny as being related to a desperately desired new life, a desire that is allied to the seasons: "Dubin's depressions repeat themselves with the regularity of the seasonal cycle. During the time span of the novel—two and a half years—each winter Dubin undergoes a psychological death and each spring, with the advent of Fanny into his life, a resurrection."[7]

Attempting to fight death through passion rather than through the intellect as he has been doing, Dubin misuses Lawrence's ideas. For Lawrence, sexual passion was not a way of avoiding death but of changing consciousness and renewing ties to the true sources of being: the instinctual, spontaneous, blood self and not the controlling mind. The individual must see himself as part of nature and its cycles and not merely as an observer of them. While Dubin understands that Fanny is connecting him with these deeper sources, he can only go so far. The reason for this is perceptively observed by Daniel Fuchs, when he states that "in Malamud the emphasis is not on the consequent Dionysian release of cosmic energies but on the moral burden passion entails. In Lawrence passion makes men, at least the male, powerful; in Malamud it makes one good, evil, or indifferent. This is why Dubin never feels a transcendent release through passion. He feels its weight" (Fuchs, 211).

The reason Malamud chose Lawrence as a subject for Dubin's bio-graphical concern is clearly not because Dubin shares a kinship with Lawrence. It has much more to do with a desire to show Dubin's weaknesses, to provide another level of characterization. Malamud said that he gave Dubin Lawrence as a subject "because Lawrence's theories about the significant relationship of sexual experience to the deeper sources of life and beyond into a kind of mystical universe gave Dubin things he could think about more than mere experience itself. . . . Lawrence's theories give the world of sex a kind of deepening" (Tyler, 32). Lawrence takes Dubin beyond the mundane world of his marriage and affair into himself, so as to show the conflict between mind and passion, words and reality.

Malamud rejected the idea of making Dubin a cellist or a painter and "lucked into making him a biographer," which he felt "opens up his life, makes him more interesting and more complex" (Tyler, 32). Consideration must now be given to the complexities of the various conflicts Dubin faces as they relate to his marriage, his affair, and his relationship to his children.

Marriage and Mistresses

Dubin's Lives focuses on the analysis of a failed marriage. While there are a number of facets to the Dubin marriage that are shared by many marriages (the need for compromise, restrictions of freedom, a lack of spontaneity), Dubin and Kitty are highly individualistic and bring to their relationship very particular problems. Dubin needs the stability of his marriage to pursue the lives of others in his biographies; however, this very stability adds to his natural tendency toward isolation from life, to his resistence to getting involved in the exigencies of the real world. Kitty suffers from aimlessness, fear of death (her constant concern with imaginary gas leaks), and an inability to place her marriage to Nathanael Willis firmly in the past. (Dubin sometimes thinks of himself as a "step-husband.") One commentator believes that "the slow disintegration of Dubin's marriage provides the best-sustained writing in the novel" (Hershinow, 117). Indeed, Malamud's portrayal of the anatomy of a marriage is frequently more effective than his depictions of the affair between Dubin and Fanny.

The lack of sensuality in his marriage is one of the factors that probably attracted Dubin to Lawrence; perhaps he could achieve an understanding of the sensual through him. Even Thoreau is related to

Dubin's need for vicarious understanding: "Marriage was his Walden—act to change his life; and what's past but persists. Change you change your past, they say" (*DL*, 87). Dubin sees his marriage as having failed to provide either "blood" knowledge or a change in his personality. He remains who he was. Obviously, his expectations of marriage have been too great, but even in his more objective moments, Dubin fails to recognize his own limitations. This may be why his wife cannot forget her first husband, who, she says, "did not resent me for needing him . . ." and "gave affection easily" (*DL*, 336).

We see Kitty through Dubin's eyes, yet when he quotes her letters it is clear that he is not wrong in presenting her as a neurotic woman with a troubled past that she cannot leave behind. Her problem with the past is similar to that suffered by many of Malamud's characters. She is careful with experience, avoiding risks if possible. However, with his own limitations Dubin cannot bring out her best. They are wrong for each other: "He felt confined by her limitations; she was diminished by his smallnesses" (*DL*, 101). When she starts an affair with Ondyk, she finds that she no longer smells the gas burners; she tells Dubin that it was on account of him that she began the affair. The marriage has not provided the basis for either of them to grow.

In Malamud's earlier novels, marriage is not presented as a living arrangement that creates happiness. It is seen as necessary for stability and the harnessing of sexual drives. It also serves to provide a structure within which characters can exercise that moral selflessness that is so central to Malamud's idea of character development. Whether Morris Bober, Frank Alpine, Sy Levin, Yakov Bok, or Harry Lesser are or would be happy in their existing or possible future marriages is highly problematic. In *Dubin's Lives* marriage is decidedly not a fulfilling state in which to live.

Women in Malamud's fiction frequently have flaws of one sort or another. As noted, Kitty has many problems that she admits to, and she is reminiscent of Pauline in *A New Life* and Irene in *The Tenants*. Like Irene, she has undergone psychoanalysis, although this does not seem to have done much good. She remains partly as she described herself in an early letter to Dubin: "I can't say my emotional season is spring but I love life. Fortunately, I have a strong reality element that keeps me balanced against some of my more neurotic inclinations" (*DL*, 47). Her characterization certainly does not stress an orientation toward loving life or balance. Indeed, she also shares some traits with Hannah Dubin, the protagonist's insane mother.[8]

Most of the female characters in Malamud's works do not have careers but instead devote themselves to the capture of a male who will fit into their plans, which usually revolve around setting up a family. Malamud is a traditionalist so far as women are concerned, and for most of his women, "biology is still destiny" (Alter 1981, 92). In *The Tenants,* Irene seems to be interested in her acting career, but she stays in New York only so long as it seems possible that either Willie or Harry will marry her. When Harry goes back to his book, she leaves. Unlike Irene, Kitty does not even consider work outside the home, except for time-filling jobs. It is only with Fanny Bick that Malamud presents a woman who seems able to pursue a life that does not involve an immediate urge for a family, though she does eventually want one. Fanny's independence is necessary because this novel is based less on a conflict between male characters than are many of Malamud's previous ones. Here Kitty and Fanny, in who they are as people and in the life-styles they represent, provide the major impetus of the novel. While both women focus attention on the protagonist and provide the most important means of understanding him, like the women in *The Natural,* they are interesting and important in their own right. They are not, as is frequently the case in such earlier works as *The Assistant, The Fixer,* and *The Tenants,* distinctly minor characters having little interest apart from the male protagonist.

Kitty remains fairly constant in her character, the decline in her relationship with her husband seeming to emerge with unfortunate ease from her troubled past. It is Fanny who shows signs of development, both because of her youth and the changed situation of women in society. Malamud remarked that "he had been influenced by the women's movement through his daughter, Janna, 'who raised my consciousness'" (Tyler, 34). Fanny's arrival in Center Campobello is no accident; she has come to seek out Dubin, whose biography of Mark Twain has convinced her that he knows things about life from which she could benefit. She wants to grow, and she certainly shows signs of developing from a slang-ridden, rather superficial young woman into someone who knows what she wants to do with her life and is in much more control of it than when we first met her. The irony of her developing at all is that she is aided by Dubin, whom we see as undeveloped in many areas and who, unlike most of Malamud's previous protagonists, "gains no wisdom and earns no 'redemption. . . .'"[9]

Fanny is open about her needs, asking Dubin about courses, careers, books, and living. She writes to him, stating: "But the truth of it is I want to be responsible, to work my life out decently"; and, "Advise me, William. I'm afraid I'll be anxious again. Tell me what to do about myself. You're so serious about life, tell me what to do with mine" (*DL,* 135, 220). With Fanny, Dubin takes on a parent's role, replacing her own inadequate father and successfully giving her advice. He also provides a father substitute for Kitty, but a much less effective one, given her problems, his limitations, and the nature of their marriage. He fails as a father to his children because of his inability to convey emotion and their knowledge of his limitations.

Fanny's growth as an individual through following and rejecting different aspects of Dubin's advice places her in the unlikely position of assistantship, like Frank Alpine to Morris Bober, Seymour Levin to Leo Duffy, and Yakov Bok to Shmuel. The important difference in this novel is that "it is the first time in Malamud's fiction that the role of inheritor, so critical a moral function in his work, has been assumed by a woman" (Alter 1981, 180). Not only does Fanny learn from Dubin, she teaches him, as well—and not merely the importance of Lawrencean sensuality. Aware that an important part of their relationship is based on Dubin's longing to regain his lost youth, Fanny lectures him: "William, everybody feels they have lost some part of their youth. I know I have, and maybe that's what it's for. Maybe if you lose it you make up by learning something you have to know—the way I imagine you have, and the way I'd like to" (*DL,* 268). She understands Dubin better than he does himself and appreciates that certain types of knowledge come only through loss, a most insightful attitude. A few pages later, Dubin bemoans the fact that he cannot even live by what he has learned.

Both Fanny and Dubin have normal human weaknesses of which they are aware, and both are attempting to come to grips with them. However, despite his more than thirty years' greater experience in living, perhaps because of his advanced age compared to hers, Dubin seems less likely to achieve a successful integration of his needs, personality, and social position (the married state, for him) than does Fanny. Also, because he cannot love anyone totally, Dubin "ends up treating both his wife and mistress badly—he will not leave Kitty for Fanny but neither will he give up Fanny" (Hershinow, 107).

Malamud's depiction of the themes engaging Dubin, Kitty, and Fanny are effectively presented, although at times there is too much repetition of emotions and insights. By contrast, the issues involving Dubin's children, Maud and Gerald, are undeveloped and seem almost tacked on to the plot, perhaps to show Dubin's ignorance of his emotional distance from the children. Because neither child is sufficiently characterized, the startling events in their lives edge into melodrama, existing only to give an injection of possible new interest to a flagging plot and to tie up the loose ends of Dubin's family life, such as it is. Neither Maud nor Gerald emerge as real people, and their situations are not entirely convincing. Both are stereotypes: pseudo-hippies who have rejected conventional behavior; Malamud seems to want to create a too-obvious generation gap that Dubin can only partially bridge with Fanny. It is notable that Maud works with Dubin on one book and then marries, choosing the conventional cure for what ails women, despite its dubious value in the novel; Gerald "grows up," eventually accepting his parents with their flaws. Neither result is expected, especially given Dubin's admitted self-centeredness.

The title contains a pun on "Lives": Dubin not only reads and writes the lives of others in order to extend his own rather unadventurous and sedentary one but he also tries out a passionate and erotic life with Fanny—Dubin "lives." This is Malamud's most sexually explicit novel, though there have been forays into the erotic in most of his previous ones. Here, however, placing Dubin under the influence of Lawrence and exposing him to the benefit of Fanny's expertise, Malamud presents the sexuality as essential to the full development of a human being. Except for the ending of *Pictures of Fidelman*, "The Glassblower of Venice," where the protagonist is redeemed, in part through sexuality, Malamud's heroes suffer for their sexual side; *Dubin's Lives* follows the pattern, as Dubin goes through the fires of the damned for his pleasures with Fanny.

Robert Towers observes that "*Dubin's Lives,* despite a couple of episodes that verge on the fantastic, is the most realistic, the least fabulous or schematic of Malamud's novels since *A New Life* . . ." (Towers, 1). After Yakov Bok's dreams and visions in *The Fixer;* Fidelman's surrealistic world in "Pictures of the Artist"; and Lesser's reveries and dreams, the junglelike apartments, and multiple endings of *The Tenants,* one might be forgiven some surprise at the conventionality of the structure of *Dubin's Lives*. Malamud's next novel, *God's Grace*, will move firmly back into the fabulous, permitting us to see *Dubin's Lives* as an hiatus in the late novels, a throwback indeed to *A New Life.*

As in his other novels, Malamud uses a concealed third-person omniscient narrator who has the benefits of standing outside and above the action yet merges with Dubin's thoughts so subtly that the transition from one voice to the other is almost invisible. The nuances of Dubin's ruminations, his interpretations of events and feelings, are central to the plot. The claustrophobia that this intense introspection inevitably creates at times is, however, mitigated by the narrator's observations.

The ending of the novel is disappointing for the same reason that Maud and Gerald's about-face is: it does not follow from what preceded it. While it shares the qualified optimism that was common to the works before *The Tenants,* the end does not really state to what conclusion Dubin or the novel has come. One commentator calls it "a half-cocked ending if there ever was one" (Fuchs, 210). Will Dubin give up Fanny? Has he regained his love for Kitty? The movement throughout the novel would seem to point to an answer of "No" to both questions, an answer that Dubin's running from Fanny with "his half-stiffened phallus in his hand, for his wife with love" (*DL,* 362) ambiguously contradicts.

What is clear is that Dubin completes his biography of Lawrence, apparently overcoming his lack of sympathetic understanding, most likely through Fanny's influence. He goes on to write two more books; whatever the result of his sexual and marital arrangements, his self-discipline remains unscathed. It is noteworthy that Dubin moves from the intuition of Lawrence to the scientific approach to understanding human beings applied by Freud's daughter Anna, the founder of child psychoanalysis. Dubin writes this biography in collaboration with Maud.

Anna Freud did fundamental work on ego psychology in which she analyzed the development of the ego's unconscious defense mechanisms, illustrating how these are used as adjustive strategies in personality development. She also studied the effects of instinctual drives on ego development and published *Ego and the Mechanisms of Defense.* Dubin's own problems with his children are reflected in Anna Freud's scientific concerns with children's inner emotional lives and in how to apply psychoanalytic theory to children and their parents. Dubin's primary difficulty in relating to children seems to lie in defenses placed around full expression of the ego. He thinks he is showing love, but this is perceived by Kitty, Maud, and Gerald as holding back, not giving freely of the self. Dubin and Maud's working together on Anna Freud's biography points to a healing of the rift between father and daughter, a growth of mutual giving and understanding.

In spite of its weaknesses, *Dubin's Lives* is a major novel that shows Malamud's ability to analyze closely the intricacies of human relationships. One critic feels that after this novel Malamud cannot be considered "an exotic miniature to be savored before the main course of American literature"; that he has "secured a place for himself in the front ranks of contemporary fiction writers" (Shechner, 184–85). I think that he achieved this status in 1967, with the award of his second National Book Award and the Pulitzer Prize for *The Fixer*. In the next chapter, I will discuss his final novel published before his death, a work of ultimate pessimism in which the universe is seen to be ruled by a God who will not tolerate man's evil but who shows Himself to possess little of the quality of pity that Malamud has been at such pains to show is essential for humankind.

Chapter Nine
God's Grace

God and Religion

God's Grace is unlike any other novel by Malamud. While he was frequently concerned with fantasy rather than strict realism, while many of his novels possess strong elements of fable or parable, and while numerous Malamud short stories are clearly fables or parables, he wrote no other novel entirely in the form of a fable, let alone a beast fable. Two of his short stories have animals as central characters: "The Jewbird" and "Talking Horse." On account of his admiration for them, a Bennington colleague arranged for these two fables to be privately printed. Malamud said: " 'I thought, why not go at a novel with animals as the major character.' Ever since Aesop, he said: it is 'the ultimate imaginative act to create a creature—no wait, there's a better word—a living being who is not human and yet can talk, giving you the opportunity of presenting a miracle in every sentence he speaks' " (Suplee, F8).

The idea of using apes in a novel occurred to Malamud around 1975, while he was working on *Dubin's Lives*[1]; however, in 1973 he wrote: "I'm also reading Jane Goodall's study of chimps, *In the Shadow of Man*" (Field 1975, 16). As a result of reading works by Goodall, Darwin, and Stephen Jay Gould, Malamud felt that his character Calvin Cohn's attempts to teach the chimps were "within the realm of possibility—so much is being done, new experiments on animals, on language in animals, in a sense I'm just taking the next step" (Suplee, F8). In keeping with his reading in anthropology and evolutionary theory, Malamud gave the name George to the one character who provides some sense of hopefulness in the novel, George being the name given by Louis Leakey to the skeleton of a human forebear that he discovered in East Africa. *God's Grace,* like the two beast fables that preceded it, focuses the reader's attention not so much on the nature of animals as on the negative aspects of humanity. It is this focus that gives the novel its depth and relevance.

Overseeing events on an island—even when not clearly present—is God. Malamud presents Him as a judge, sometimes fallible, having a slightly ironic sense of humor. God tells Cohn, the island's sole human inhabitant, that his being allowed to survive was not a serious mistake and that "I myself don't know what goes on everywhere. It is not perfection although I, of course, am perfect."[2] The universe operates by cause and effect, and because of man's own actions in destroying God's creation through thermonuclear war, God has decided to finish the job.

A major issue in the novel is where the ultimate responsibility lies for man's destruction. Much as Jews have held God to task for breaking the covenant by allowing the persecution of his "holy people," so Calvin Cohn cites chapter and verse to Him for allowing a second flood to follow the nuclear devastation, after His promise to Noah that He would never again permit one. God stresses man's failings; he was free to choose his mode of action, and consistently chose evil: "But after I had created man I did not know how he would fail me next, in what manner of violence, corruption, blasphemy, beastliness, sin beyond belief. Thus he defiled himself. I had not foreseen the extent of it" (*GG,* 4–5). Not only did God make a mistake in leaving Cohn alive, but he was not capable of foreseeing the actions of the creatures He created. Having given man free will, He simply left him to hang himself.

The issue of free will has long been important theologically, for without it considerations of morality would be impossible. If human beings lacked free will, they could not be held responsible for their actions; they would have to act in ways determined by an outside force or by their own unchangeable natures. Despite His stating that He gave man free will, God implies that He could have done something to prevent man from destroying himself if He had chosen to, but He had had enough of the perverse creature He had created: "Therefore I let them do away with themselves. They invented the manner; I turned my head" (*GG,* 5). If God had not "turned His head," might He have been able to stop the nuclear holocaust, to change man's heart? Malamud appears to want it both ways.

For Calvin Cohn the issue is clear: "God made us who we are" (*GG,* 6); that is, it is God's fault. Later, he wonders: "Never mind free will. How can the mind be free if the mind is limited by its constitution? Why hadn't the Almighty—in sum—done a better job, . . . endowed him with a little more control over his instincts . . . ?" (*GG,* 135).

Why indeed? Cohn surely has a point, and Malamud is at pains to establish that God is not man and cannot understand man. His answer to Cohn's protest is much the same as the answer given to Job: "Who are you to understand the Lord's intention?" (*GG,* 136). Sidney Richman observes that God "may even appear demonic, break the covenant at will, and plunge the world into immitigable woe. In the presence of such a Mystery man can only surrender in silence."[3]

If God appears to have such limited positive feelings toward man, why, Cohn wonders, did He create him in the first place? He did not show his "face" even to Moses but seems to desire worship and to talk to humans. Cohn recalls the answers given by some of the sages of the past, that man would "reflect His light" and assure Him that "He was present." He wanted to "create justice on earth . . . " but his creation was "insufficient" (*GG*, 39). God tells Cohn that He "created man to perfect Himself" (*GG*, 137). In permitting man self-destruction God lessened Himself, and there is a decided tone of disappointment in Malamud's presentation of God's angry voice.

God is interested in all of humankind, not only the Jews. He tells Cohn, "I am not a tribal God; I am Master of the Universe" (*GG*, 6). Although Cohn attempts to establish Judaism as the religion of the island, resisting the Christianity that Buz was taught by Dr. Bünder, it is clear that God does not consider Judaism to be the only religion worthy of His approbation. While humans have been unable to live up to the demands of any religion, religion itself is not condemned.

The God who appears so harsh to Cohn nevertheless allows him to survive, even after His initial error. Cohn actually blesses God and believes Him capable of mercy, an attitude that will vary as his mood and the circumstances change. Despite the fact that God occasionally helps Cohn, Claude Rawson comments that "He is the pointed opposite of Crusoe's God, a source of perpetual discomfort rather than reassurance."[4] It is with this highly problematical God that Calvin Cohn must cope and under the "eye" of whom he must try to develop a religion for himself and the other primate survivors.

Cohn was on the sea floor when the Devastation struck. He was always interested in First Causes, in life's beginnings, and had even studied for the rabbinnate. Yet he is skeptical about God's goodness, fearing more than loving Him—particularly after the second flood. To survive, he believes that he must win God's favor, and that a good way of doing so might be to create a civilized social community on the island. Thus, Cohn's attempts to recreate among the chimps the best of human society has as much to do with self-preservation as altruism. He dreams of a new start, with himself as the progenitor of a new religious life: "If this small community behaved, developed, endured, it might someday—if some chimpy Father Abraham got himself born—produce its own Covenant with God" (*GG*, 128). Perhaps the chimps could succeed where men failed.

The religion Cohn attempts to teach to the chimps is his own. He will not tolerate Buz's ideas about Jesus and God being love. Cohn believes, but reluctantly; Buz, being much simpler, believes simply. Despite toasting freedom of religion at the seder, it does not exist on Cohn's island, and eventually Buz decides to change Cohn's admonition from his resistant "God is not love . . ." (*GG*, 171) to "God is love . . ." (*GG*, 204). After all, in response to Cohn's question "What can we do to dispel the evil rife in this land," we are told that "Buz said it was Cohn's fault for not teaching love" (*GG*, 203). Although there is a substantial Judaic element in Cohn's teaching, he is primarily concerned with social relations, with ethics based on mutual benefit. Apparently, however, this is insufficient to create a viable society. Because of Cohn's severe doubts of God's love (understandable, given the Holocaust, nuclear war, and the second flood) he cannot preach spiritual truths convincingly. Even when he thanks God "for what good He did, not for what He did badly. . . . You and I are alive . . ." (*GG*, 113), there is a sense of self-preservation in his words that Buz's statements of belief lack.

In this novel, as in so many of Malamud's others, the father-son theme is important. Malamud relates this theme through Cohn's relationship to Buz; through his fatherly, almost godlike attitude toward the monkeys; and through the story of the *Akedah,* the binding of Isaac. Buz asks Cohn on four occasions to tell him this story and, not surprisingly, given that he is a chimpanzee, has difficulty grasping all its implications, especially when applying his Christian training. Of course, humans also have had difficulty understanding the full implications of the story, and Buz takes the Christian view that Isaac was killed, sacrificed, that Abraham "cut his little boy's throat . . ." (*GG*, 71). Elie Wiesel observes that "in Christianity: the threat hanging over Isaac is seen as a prefiguration of the crucifixion. Except that on Mount Moriah the act was *not* consummated: the father did *not* abandon his son. Such is the difference between Moriah and Golgotha."[5]

Buz's concern must include the fear that his "father," Cohn, might treat him as he thinks Abraham treated his son. Cohn does tell Buz that while Abraham came down from the mountain, Isaac did not. He tells him that the philosopher Kierkegaard thought that Abraham really desired to kill Isaac and explains that Kierkegaard's idea and the reason people have persisted in seeing Abraham as killing Isaac says "something about the nature of man—his fantasies of death that get enacted into the slaughter of man by man . . ." (*GG,* 74–75). It is not surprising that Buz is nervous, particularly as Cohn points out that the story shows God preferring animal to human sacrifice, this being a civilizing development. As Buz later tells Cohn, he has always been a "vegetorion."

The irony is that the novel ends not with the father binding—let alone killing—the son, but with the son killing the father in a parodic sacrifice. This shows the victory of Buz's Christian beliefs concerning sacrifice over Cohn's Judaic ones; in fact, "Cohn is sacrificed as Isaac and Jesus" (Helterman 1985, 19). While there is no Oedipal theme here, there being no mother present, there is a "wife," in Mary Madelyn, and sexual competition between "father" and "son" for the only available young female is intense. We do not see the father desiring to destroy the son, but there is the more Freudian and mythical theme of the son's desire to replace the father as the primary male and so gain sexual primacy and authority. This desire of the young male to replace or even destroy father figures exists as a theme in earlier Malamud novels, particularly in the first four.

One interpretation of Isaac's not descending the mountain is that "Isaac, unlike Abraham, was no longer the same person, that the real Isaac remained there, on the altar" (Wiesel, 97); also, that Isaac was detached spiritually from his father. Abraham showed qualities of obedience, faith, and devotion to God; he was willing to risk the loss of his beloved son to a deity in whom he believed absolutely. Cohn will help turn Buz against him through his own rigidity and his inability to respect his "son's" needs and beliefs; Cohn is no Abraham. Despite man's failure to live up to his spiritual possibilities, Cohn assumes man to be superior to animals, but in fact, Buz's ideas are frequently superior to Cohn's.

There is the possibility of seeing God in a somewhat positive light here, in that God may have known that Abraham would obey Him and that Isaac was therefore safe, the test being to confirm further Abraham's faith that God would not desert him. This possible mercy can also be seen at the end of the novel, when God has permitted Cohn to live not for just "a few deep breaths," as He stated at the beginning, but to an old age, as evidenced by Cohn's long white beard. Of course, it cannot be known how long a "breath" is to God, but He has clearly allowed Cohn time to "compose yourself, make your peace" (*GG,* 6). He has even provided George the gorilla, as a true disciple of Cohn's, who says Kaddish for his dead teacher. That his blood "spurted forth an instant before the knife touched Cohn's flesh" (*GG,* 223) shows that God is in control of events and so may have approved of some of Cohn's attempts to create a caring society, in spite of Cohn's prejudices in favor of man's ways.

Cohn has been highly critical of God, but at the end of his life he calls Him merciful for allowing him a long life. He also has mixed feelings toward his cantor father, perhaps thinking that in this case it is he, Calvin Cohn, who has failed his father "by giving up his rabbinical studies, by changing his own name, and by losing his faith" (Helterman 1985, 121). Cohn's reaction to hearing the records of his father chanting prayers full of "passion for God, pity for the world, compassion for mankind" (*GG*, 57) is one of love and attachment, perhaps not that different from his ultimate feeling for God himself. He has fled from both fathers and, in the end, returned to both.

Men and Monkeys

While the relationship between Cohn and God is very important, perhaps of greater importance in the novel is that between Cohn and the other primate survivors of the Day of Devastation. The issue of language is critical in both relationships: Cohn could not have spoken to God, nor could the chimps have communicated with Cohn, without language. Malamud raises the value of language above that of communication alone; Cohn reflects that "maybe God had invented language. The word began the world. Nor would anyone have known there was a monotheistic God if he hadn't proclaimed it'" (*GG*, 68). He later thinks: "God was Torah. He was made of words" (*GG*, 92). Language is almost holy, and even God becomes less, perhaps even losing his existence so far as humankind is concerned, without it.

Cohn has had to revise his original idea that it was man who invented language, and it was that invention that had made him superior to the rest of creation. Buz's comment, "If he was so superior where is he now?" (*GG*, 68) is unanswerable and points to a basic flaw in Cohn's feeling that language improves people, that through it, "man becomes more finely and subtly man—a sensitive, principled, civilized human being . . ." (*GG*, 69). To Buz's query as to what a human is, Cohn responds in grandiose terms: "Cohn said he thought to be human was to be responsive to and protective of life and civilization. Buz said he would rather be a chimp" (*GG*, 70). Given the evidence of the results of man's behavior toward his own species, who can say that Buz is wrong? Cohn does not see it this way, though, and never loses faith in the civilizing effects of language, the great possibilities for humankind, and the desirability of making the chimps as human as possible while ignoring what their experience as animals has taught them.

Starting with the idea that the chimps are merely incipient humans, Cohn places his faith in language to bring them to their highest development. The moral power of language is seen not only in its relation to God, to words and the word, but in terms of Cohn's need for belief when he discovers that Buz can speak, and the chimp tells him that all animals do, Cohn need only admit the possibility: "Belief itself may not be that easy, but I want to believe" (*GG,* 66). Buz refers to Cohn's need to "hov faith" and later to the chimps having learned to speak because they had faith. Cohn sees speech as providing a similar purpose for him as did the creation of man for God: ". . . I hear my own voice and know I am present" (*GG,* 55). Thus for Cohn speech equals existence and a tie to a deeply flawed humanity, and to at least a partial understanding of the nature of God. Having placed so many attributes upon it, however, he is bound to be disappointed in what it can achieve.

An early sign that Cohn views words not only as an opportunity for advancement and civilization but also for control and status occurs when he decides to change Gottlob's name to Buz. In replacing Dr. Bünder as the chimp's "father" and teacher, Cohn simply informs him of his new name, and when the chimp becomes angry, he assumes him to be temperamental. He becomes cross when Buz begins naming the new chimps, because Cohn has taken on Adam's role, "somehow forgetting that he is the last man instead of the first" (Helterman 1985, 110). Buz's choice of names is biblical; the gentler chimps receive New Testament names whereas the aggressive Esau receives his from the Hebrew Bible. This shows Buz's preference for Christianity, a form of which he will return to at the end of the novel.

The society that Cohn wishes to establish is one that is vegetarian, practices kindness to all, shares food equally, and views all living beings as having value. Unfortunately, animal and human nature do not permit this ideal to be realized. Cohn cannot get Buz to accept George, and he even threatens to kill the gorilla himself after George destroys one of Cohn's records. As Buz reminds him, it was Cohn who said love did not work before the second flood, so why should it now? The monkeys begin and end their relationship not by sharing but by the strongest male taking first what he wants. As with humans, altruistic behavior takes a far second place to behavior based on nature. Cohn never pays sufficient attention to the demands of animal nature, particularly when it suits his own interests not to. When Buz wishes to mate with Mary Madelyn, he tells Cohn, who has appropriated her, that she is his kind, not Cohn's. Cohn eliminates this completely reasonable remark by saying that "on this island there was only one kind—sentient, intelligent living beings" (*GG,* 157). Cohn tells Esau to masturbate and leave Mary alone. By teaching her human language, and reading to her from *Romeo and Juliet,* Cohn removes her from the natural world where she belongs. The male chimps who pursue her are justifiably puzzled and angry as, despite the fact that she is in heat, she runs terrified from them desiring a Shakespearean form of romantic love that only Cohn understands. In the end the monkeys rebel and overcome Cohn, and Mary becomes a normal chimp again.

Cohn can be admired for attempting to overcome the baser natures of the monkeys. This is, after all, what the ideal of civilization is about: suppressing or rechanneling basic nature for a "higher" goal, that of individual achievement or the good of the larger society. However, even with humans, who are presumably farther up the evolutionary scale than monkeys, this suppression cannot be too extensive, and outlets must be provided. Bertrand Russell pointed out that a successful society will create areas, allow room, where basic drives can be expressed in a socially acceptable manner. Cohn's island society allows no outlet for the monkey's sexual drives or aggressive instincts. This, combined with his imposed religious, philosophical, and sociological ideas helps to explain his created society's failure.

Early in his stay on the island, we see that Cohn fails to appreciate the power of "nature." He brings a rifle with him when exploring the island, and to his credit does realize that its presence there constitutes "a stupid fear, really atavistic. It should have gone with the Devastation, but somehow persisted" (*GG,* 83). Whenever he fires a bullet to practice, Buz runs and hides. The key fact here is that his fear "somehow persisted." Cohn never comes to grips with the "somehow" of his own nature, despite his clear-sighted understanding of human nature in general.

He lectures the chimps on man's ambivalent nature and insufficiency, his "no-in-yes, evil-in-good . . ." (*GG,* 132). He tells them that for man "love is not a popular phenomenon . . . he never mastered his animal nature for the good of all . . ." (*GG,* 133). If man was unable to master his animal nature, how can animals be expected to master theirs? Nonetheless, Cohn dreams of a chimpanzee society that will not repeat man's errors. Is this admirable or simply foolish? Cohn brings his own dreams—and flaws—to the experiment.

As a scientist, Cohn uses his knowledge of evolution to hope for a brighter future. Chimps are like men, he believes: they can be nasty but are basically affectionate; with luck they might develop into more moral beings than man, and God would favor them. If he mates with Mary, he might help evolution along by creating a creature that would combine the best of man and monkey—man's brain with a chimp's affection. The idea is mad, but not wholly mad. That it ends in disaster reveals the level of pessimism that Malamud—steadily moving toward this stance in his writing—has reached.

Cohn's Admonitions—altruism as wish-fulfillment—are quickly followed by the wall he builds to seal the mouth of his cave dwelling against the possible danger posed by outsiders—altruism as reality. After Rebekah's murder, Cohn clips the wires that permit Buz human speech. Given the value that Cohn has placed upon language, this is an extremely violent act and an admission of the inadequacy of human speech to humanize, in the best sense of that word. Buz is aware of the enormity of Cohn's act, and after stating that he is innocent of any crime, says that Dr. Bünder would never do that to him because "he loved me as a father loves his child" (*GG,* 215). His last word is "Gottlob," the name Dr. Bünder gave him and which he returns to, rejecting Cohn's Buz. When Buz loses his speech, the other chimps lose theirs too, symbolizing their complete abandonment of the human world following the "dehumanization" of Buz, who had taught them speech and preached to them.

Although Buz is the most important monkey in the novel, Esau heightens some of the conflicts Cohn has with Buz and permits Malamud to bring forth other issues related to the problems in any society. Although Buz has a spiritual sense that Esau lacks, he agrees with him concerning Mary. Cohn sees Esau as a disruptive element in his plans for a perfect community and considers getting rid of him because of his constant pursuit of Mary. Buz points out Mary's unnaturalness and suggests that they get rid of her. Esau is correct in blaming Cohn's teachings for Mary's resistance to the males, and he sums up the problem when he resists Cohn's desire to have all the chimps working: "'Why disturb yourself if the fruit is for free? Why spoil our natures to please a non-chimp? Who is he, for instance?' Cohn wouldn't say" (*GG,* 147). Although Esau is undoubtedly an objectionable character, his criticisms are sound, and Cohn seems aware that he is not on entirely firm ground.

When Esau kills and devours the baby baboon Sara, Cohn holds a funeral and lectures the chimps on the value of life. Again, Esau points out that it is natural to hunt small baboons who "don't belong to our tribe . . . ," this hunt fulfilling part of what chimpanzees are. It is noteworthy that even the half-human child Rebekah eats the head of her doll, reminiscent of Esau savoring the taste of Sara's brain.

Esau, whom Cohn sees as the outsider, the other, shifts the ground so that Cohn becomes the outsider, the Jew. Cohn sees those on the island as Jews in history. To Buz's question, "Who are we?" Cohn answers: "The still-alive—those who have survived despite the terrible odds . . ." (*GG*, 121). In this scenario, Esau becomes a part of the majority, and an anti-Semite. He justifies killing baboons not only on the basis of chimpanzee instinct but in terms that hark back to Nazi propaganda about Jews: they are dirty, thieving, too fecund, and want special privileges. Sexual envy is, of course, also a factor. "You possessed my betrothed and forced her to bear your half-breed child. I will break every Jewbone in your head" (*GG*, 201). In the end Esau wins, and the only actual Jew on the island is destroyed, in a reversal of the biblical story. Here, "it is Esau rather than Jacob who gets his father's birthright" (Helterman 1985, 108), and we recall the name of Cohn's ship, the *Rebekah Q*, Rebekah having been mother to both Jacob and Esau. The *Rebekah Q* saved Cohn/Jacob and Buz, who later took on Esau's role by replacing him as the Alpha Ape. Thus, Cohn's desire to create a civilization based on Judaic control of instinct fails. The one remaining hope for the future lies in George the gorilla.

George is a mysterious creature who early on shows signs of morality. It is he who saves Cohn's life by bringing him food and drink when he is ill, and he responds dramatically to the sound of Cohn's father saying Kaddish, a foreshadowing of the "long Kaddish" that he, wearing a yarmulke, will say for Cohn after his death. Cohn feels that there are hidden depths to George, that his appearance hides his gentleness. Sidney Richman comments that he suspects that "the deeper possibilities Malamud sees in George—or at least those that set him apart from the chimps—have to do with the fact that gorillas *can* cry and chimps cannot and that, further, gorilla fathers are caring fathers and chimps are not" (Richman 1987, 219). This places gorillas in a closer relationship to humans than are chimpanzees, and George's rejection by the chimps, who—given Buz's preaching—may be viewed as a possible Christian majority in the novel, parallels their rejection of Cohn and his "Jewish" philosophy.

George goes off on his own to reflect on things that Cohn says. He also leaves for a time after two baboons are killed and eaten. His inability to develop speech as fast as the chimpanzees may have to do with his need to grasp certain moral and religious ideas first, so that speech truly is a civilizing quality for him. He becomes his teacher's only true follower: "At the end, in a direct counter to Buz's crime, Cohn and *his* father and *his* find their immortality as George finds his tongue . . . and so the message of piety and redemption is passed down without scar or break" (Richman 1987, 219).

Form

The major literary influences and allusions in the novel are to the Hebrew Bible, *The Life and Strange Surprizing Adventures of Robinson Crusoe,* and *The Tempest.* Also important are *Gulliver's Travels, Lord of the Flies,* and *Animal Farm,* with shades of *Dr. Doolittle* and Aesop's *Fables.* The focus in the Bible is on Genesis: the novel is divided into six sections, (perhaps pointedly no seventh day of rest occurs after a successful creation), and in addition to the stories of the Flood and the *Akedah,* there is an Adam and Eve tale that ends in disaster. Clearly God's intentions on Cohn's Island are different from those He had in the Bible, as the trial of belief is much more difficult in the novel.

In comparison with *God's Grace, Robinson Crusoe,* like Genesis, "provides a set of expectations, both for Cohn and the reader, none of which are fulfilled (save for the revolting feast). . . ."[6] Defoe's novel concludes on an optimistic note, a very different ending from Malamud's: "Crusoe's Friday is converted from his cannibal ways, while Cohn's subjects 'revert' to them; it is arguable that both processes are the result of the White Man's educational project. . . . So a teasing question-mark hovers over whether the cannibal acts are mainly to be seen as features of their human or their simian nature" (Rawson, 10).

While this question receives no unambiguous answer in *God's Grace,* Malamud's pessimism is clear. He called the novel "a visionary tale with a prophetic warning"[7] and said, "I am more pessimistic than I used to be. . . . Man seems to be a constant disappointment to himself" (Benedict, 36). Just as Prospero in *The Tempest* fails in his attempt to impose an ideal set of laws on Caliban's Island, largely because he ignores the views of its only inhabitant, so Cohn's experiment ends in disastrous disappointment because of his human pride in thinking man is superior to all other life forms, despite the glaring evidence of human failure. In trying to be not only Prospero but also like God, Cohn disregards the deeply flawed nature of man, although he is certainly aware of it.

Cohn's dreams about an albino ape tell us of fears that he will not admit. Cohn fears that man is just an ape, with apelike qualities. This is clearly symbolized when the ape, in Cohn's imagination, takes a black mask from Cohn's face and places it in front of his own, in effect becoming Cohn. Buz has commented: "A white ape, they can be nasty people" (*GG*, 154). When Cohn spears the white ape, he "felt as though he had murdered a man" (*GG*, 214). What he has tried to murder is his alter ego, which is telling him that man is no different from other primates. However, if he accepted this he could not place man in a superior position in relation to the other denizens of the island. Also, he would have to believe truly—not just say it, but believe it—that, given man's history and the nuclear holocaust that men visited on the world, the apes and monkeys may really be worth listening to, despite their bestial qualities that, like man's, remain stubbornly resistant to change. At least they did not utterly destroy each other.

Malamud said that he was long concerned with the nuclear danger facing the world, and what that said about humankind: "I have a sense now, as many people have, of peril—it's terribly frightening. I feel it is the writer's business to cry havoc, because silence can't increase understanding or evoke mercy" (Benedict, 28). The Nazi Holocaust is also raised in this novel, another example of the horrendous possibilities contained within the human animal. Malamud bemoaned the fact that "we haven't conquered some of our major evils—racial hatred, bigotry, intolerance" (Suplee, F8). The result of this inability of man's to understand and control his baser drives is, in *God's Grace,* his complete destruction, an end even bleaker than that of *The Tenants,* which at least contained two possible optimistic endings, though the pessimistic one was the more likely.

In *The Tenants,* the tenement in which Lesser and Spearmint play out their drama is referred to as an "accursed island," and in both novels the protagonist's possessions and home are destroyed by an Esau/Ishmael with whom he fails to relate on a level of common purpose and destiny: "Like *The Tenants* before it *God's Grace* wonders why well-meaning people cannot live together in peace, even if they are of different persuasions" (Sinclair, 1188). In both novels, the immediate cause of the animosity is not intellectual or philosophical but much more basic: both protagonists gain the sexual favors of a female that their antagonists consider rightfully theirs. However, "Lesser's words ['Anti-Semitic Ape'] become literally true when Cohn in his turn, is set upon by Esau . . ." (Sinclair, 1188).

Several critics have found the novel unsatisfactory, referring to it as Walt Disney-ish and calling the chimps clichéd and corny. One commentator finds Mary too "stereotypically feminine . . . fluff-headed . . . all pout and lisp. . . ." She also notes that Malamud takes risks with her in that "her sex scenes with Cohn are bound to raise a few horrified eyebrows among readers, incidentally. They may even get the book banned, along with *The Fixer,* where the Moral Majority holds sway" (Benedict, 31).

More common have been reactions like John Updike's, that "Malamud's curious sensual searchingness bestows upon the apes such individuality that the reader can almost tell them apart by smell."[8] The language through which Malamud presents the monkeys has been seen as largely effective in its comedy and frivolity, and in that it makes readers pay close attention to the dialogue because of the oddness of the device. One writer has referred to the novel as "trenchant moral satire."[9]

God's Grace is most effective in the way that Malamud skillfully manages the essential requirement of satire, that it combine education with comedy, that comedy be used as a weapon against human vice and folly. Cohn's remarks and Buz's rejoinders frequently remind us that we are dealing here with the last man on earth and a talking chimpanzee. The novel is loaded with ironic overtones, the most extreme being the possibility of finding room for laughter amid the disasters that have overtaken humankind in the novel. Malamud was very much aware of this: "Even a reader of holocaust drama has to be enticed into the act of reading, or he may feel he would rather forgo the anguish. . . . Not all of us are eager to be reminded of how close man has come, through his own madness, to the end of time. So, I wanted a little laughter in this serious book" (Benedict, 30).

The bittersweet humor is very much in the Jewish vein that we have seen in *The Assistant* and *The Fixer,* both also concerned with somber themes. God's speech patterns touch Yiddish intonations, and, despite his fear, there is a sense at times of a Jewish family spat going on between Cohn and God, with God occasionally reminding Cohn of his place with a shower of pebbles and rocks. Would Malamud argue with God if he were in Cohn's position? "Of course I would! There's a whole tradition of back-talk from Adam to Job. God may not enjoy man as much as we would like Him to, but He seems to enjoy the human voice" (Benedict, 31).

Cohn follows in the footsteps of Seymour Levin in *A New Life* in changing his name, not by accident, from one that implies "seeing" to something quite different: Calvin, the name of one of the major figures of the Protestent Reformation and a stringent authoritarian, which Cohn himself becomes. One critic has used this name change as the basis of an "outrageous pun": "Instead of Calvin Klein, maker of designer jeans, Malamud gives us Calvin Cohn, creator of designer genes" (Helterman 1985, 117); so much for Rebekah, Cohn's chimp "wife," a new chance for humankind.

In the end, neither Judaism nor Christianity makes living creatures better, and there is a definite anti-Christian tone to the work in that the "Christianized" chimps sacrifice Cohn, something that Abraham never did to Isaac. Of course God told Cohn at the outset that he should not have remained alive anyway, as man was condemned to destruction; but the method Malamud uses to end Cohn's life (even given that God does the killing before Buz manages to), shows that Buz's preaching has not been effective in teaching the chimps the value of life. Do any values remain? Is there any grace from God? Malamud thought that the answer to both questions was yes: "One of the misreadings of the novel . . . is that it ends in tragedy. Some reviewers have failed to recognize that a gorilla recites Kaddish for Calvin Cohn, and that is indeed a cause for optimism; the prayer itself is a vehicle of God's Grace."[10] God continues to exist and not as a tribal God, but as one whose message can live in a nonhuman creature. God will live on in George, though what his future is—only God knows.

Chapter Ten
The Short Stories

Malamud wrote over fifty short stories during his lifetime. He said that he liked the form as much as the novel and wrote stories between novels "to breathe, and give myself time to think what's in the next book. Sometimes I'll try out a character or situation similar to that in a new novel" (Stern, 62). Some readers have felt that Malamud is at his best in the short-story form, that it is "the purest distillation of his abiding leitmotif: the still, sad music of humanity. . . . [H]is novels hold the note of sorrow too long, until what had begun as a lamentation ends as a *kvetch* [complaint]. But in the short story, Malamud achieves an almost psalmlike compression."[1]

Except perhaps in *The Fixer* and *Dubin's Lives,* it would be difficult to justify saying that Malamud's novels "hold the note of sorrow too long" and lapse into nothing more than a complaint. While the themes he explores in his novels can be seen in the stories he wrote during the course of almost forty-five years, their development is necessarily limited by the form, and even Malamud himself said that he would use the stories as laboratories for characters and ideas that he might then develop in a novel. However, the stories possess a unique quality in which some of his most effective writing can be seen.

Early Stories

Before the publication of *The Assistant* (1957), Malamud wrote nine stories that were set in small, prisonlike stores of various kinds: "Armistice," "The Grocery Store," "Riding Pants," "The Cost of Living," "The First Seven Years," "The Prison," "The Death of Me," "The Bill," and "The Loan." The first three were not published anywhere until 1989, when Malamud's uncollected stories appeared in a single volume; the other six appeared in magazines and were collected in either *The Magic Barrel* (1958) or *Idiots First* (1963); five of the six (all but "The Prison") also appear in *The Stories of Bernard Malamud* (1983).[2]

"The Cost of Living" was the first story for which Malamud was paid.

It depicts a poor grocer who, despite working 16-hour days, eventually fails and must close his store. There is no redemption, no Frank Alpine, although characters that parallel Morris, Ida, and Karp appear, and the grocer fears the same fate that overcomes Breitbart in *The Assistant*.

In "The First Seven Years," which also reflects *The Assistant,* Miriam rejects Max, a brother "materialist" to Nat Pearl, for the impoverished shoemaker Sobel, who has a soul. Sobel teaches Feld, who achieves moral growth through accepting Sobel's worth. As Helen inspires Frank, so Miriam, Feld's daughter, gives Sobel a reason for his life—love. Sobel can then go on to work for two more years before claiming Miriam, in a loose allusion to the biblical story of Jacob's having to work for Laban in order to claim Rachel. In a similar manner, Frank has to earn Helen through work and sacrifice.

The final four tales all stress the need to "give credit" to human beings, a quality that Frank learns from Morris. There is no assurance that giving credit will bring either worldly success or a human response, but it is necessary if a person is to become truly human in Malamud's world. Tommy in "The Prison" learns from his own suffering in the candy store and tries to save a young girl from becoming a thief, something she does not thank him for. Josip and Emilio in "The Death of Me" never learn the lesson of tolerance and compassion that Marcus tries to teach them. In the end, it is Marcus who is destroyed, significantly, through a heart attack. In "The Bill," Willy shows qualities of the early and later Frank Alpine in his development from one who takes to one who realizes the importance of repaying debts—financial and moral. Unlike Frank, Willy never manages to repay his debt, but through his suffering he learns what it is that one person owes to another. In "The Loan" Bessie, an early Ida Bober, permits her tragic past to make giving human credit impossible. Her fear of destitution overwhelms Lieb's desire to give to Kobotsky, although Lieb is still able to express his humanity through forgiving an old wound and giving customers his bread, into which he has shed tears representing the suffering of life.

These stories lack complexity, but it is their very carefully crafted simplicity that heightens the effectiveness of the epiphany that so frequently occurs in Malamud's tales. They also illustrate the fact that "in most of his fictions, there is at least one character who provides 'the test,' who brings the lingering internal question to the surface, who focuses the central character to the question of conscience . . ." (Benson, 21–22). In these store-based tales, providing goods or a service to others is transmuted into the need to provide human understanding and compassion for suffering human beings. The process of furnishing sustenance for the body (groceries, bread, meat, candy, or clothing) is secondary to furnishing sustenance for the spirit. The protagonists frequently become not storekeepers but keepers of the essence of what it means to be human in its highest, most altruistic and sympathetic form. All the characters "have occupations, but rarely have functions other than their relations with another person. . . . [T]heir work becomes a metaphor for their emotions or sometimes the emotion itself" (Helterman 1985, 125).

Short Story Collections

The best stories of the first 18 years of Malamud's career were collected in *The Magic Barrel,* about which the judges who awarded it the National Book Award said, "it captures the poetry of human relations at the point where imagination and reality meet."[3] The title story is the best of the collection, followed by "Angel Levine," "The First Seven Years," "The Mourners," "The Bill," and "The Loan." All these tales contain Jewish (or in "The Bill," Jewish-type) characters who must come to grips with a human debt that they must recognize and attempt to pay. Often the stories contain Yiddish dialect or cadences and are fables or parables related in form to the folktale. Some are close to the parables of Kafka in their stress on suffering leading to a moral insight. Their simplicity of structure belies their richness of insight into the human condition. The weaker stories lack a Jewish or Jewish-type character—that is, one who has a "sense of the pertinacity of spirit, an indefinable aura of 'goodness' which . . . transforms the most extreme of failures into a sad redemption" (Richman, 111).

Malamud's second collection of stories, *Idiot's First,* was published in 1963 and did not achieve the same standard as *The Magic Barrel,* but in "The German Refugee" it does treat with more depth the subject of the Holocaust, which is touched upon in the earlier collection in "The Lady of the Lake." The best tales—"Idiots First," "The Death of Me," "The Jewbird," and "The German Refugee"—are very impressive and reveal concerns similar to those of the earlier volume. The form has been altered, however, with only "The Death of Me" closely following the style of the earlier simply written parables with epiphanies that stress the possibility of redemption through suffering. Both "Idiots First" and "The Jewbird" show continuing skill in the use of fantasy.

The stories in *Rembrandt's Hat,* which was published in 1973, date from the late sixties and early seventies and veer strongly toward pessimism. While a majority of the tales in *The Magic Barrel* can be called optimistic, the opposite is so in the second collection *Idiots First.* The most impressive tales in *Rembrandt's Hat* are "The Silver Crown," "Man in the Drawer" (the longest short story Malamud wrote), and "Talking Horse." "The Letter" and "My Son the Murderer" show Malamud experimenting with new forms, in the latter tale, with point-of-view. In most of the stories in *Rembrandt's Hat,* the characters find it very difficult or impossible to express mercy, compassion, or charity, and the distance between fathers and sons is a common theme.

In addition to many others, all of Malamud's best tales were collected in *The Stories of Bernard Malamud,* published in 1983. The less impressive stories that he chose not to include in his earlier collections were brought together and published posthumously in *The People and Uncollected Stories,* a useful volume that also contains an unfinished novel, which will be discussed in Chapter 11.

Italian Tales

In addition to the six stories collected in *Pictures of Fidelman* (see Chapter 6), Malamud wrote five other Italian stories: "The Elevator," "The Lady of the Lake," "Behold the Key," "The Maid's Shoes," and "Life Is Better than Death." Although these tales share many themes with those set in an American urban center, Italy, with its distinctive history and character, provides an ambience different than that of Malamud's claustrophobic stores and rundown New York streets. Nevertheless the characters in the stories set in Italy, American or Italian, are similar to the New Yorkers in their suffering, their need to receive and difficulty in giving "credit," and their sense of imprisonment in the past.

"The Elevator," "Behold the Key," and "The Maid's Shoes" present the theme of Americans' inability to appreciate the difficulties of Italians. The American protagonists, George Agostini, Carl Schnieder, and Orlando Krantz, view Italians through American eyes and apply American standards to Italian behavior and culture. None has suffered greatly and so they cannot understand the attitudes of Italian characters, the Signora, Bevilacqua, De Vecchis, and the maid.

In "The Elevator" Eleonora is an Italian version of the suffering storekeepers and their assistants in the New York tales, and she brings forth compassion from George, who cannot understand that the Signora holds on to her control over the use of the elevator as one of the last privileges left to her in postwar Italian society. Having lost the respect of the lower classes, the Signora cannot appreciate Eleonora's plight, and Eleonora flaunts her new power at the end of the story by riding up and down, over and over, perhaps simply overjoyed by this small improvement in her wretched life.

Like George, Carl cannot grasp the social complexities of the situation in "Behold the Key." He sees Italy through a romantic haze and is unprepared for the desperation of Italians simply trying to make a living. The key that brands him at the end may prove to be the key to any understanding he will gain as a limited "student of Italian life and manners"; his inability to see Italians as suffering human beings rather than something to be studied leads to his failure. Bevilacqua and De Vecchis represent Italians who "may legitimately be considered as strongly recommended candidates for promotion to that dubious grace, Jewishness as suffering. . . ."[4]

Similar to Carl, Krantz, in "The Maid's Shoes," is uninterested in involvement with Italians, preferring books to real life. An "authority in law," he refuses communication with the maid until severely pressed, thus committing a serious sin for a Malamud character, who cannot grow morally unless he can transcend himself and show genuine compassion for the suffering of others. Richman considers this tale Malamud's "most successful attempt to extend the distinctive concerns of the Jewish stories into non-Jewish characters in a non-Jewish world" (Richman, 133).

"Life Is Better Than Death" is the only Italian story that contains neither Americans nor Jews of any nationality, and perhaps because of this, a basic conflict is missing, and the story never comes to life. The ending is without hope: neither Etta nor Cesare shows any development toward a greater understanding of life. Cesare betrays, and the "life in her belly" is insufficient to turn Etta away from the sense of sin imposed on her by Italian cultural norms.

A much more successful story is "The Lady of the Lake," which brings together Italian and Jewish themes directly. Like Christopher Newman in James's *The American,* Henry Levin is an innocent abroad, but unlike Newman, Levin is ashamed of who he is—a Jew. His attempt to negate his identity and achieve happiness by changing his name to Freeman is doomed, since for Malamud, a character's identity or past cannot be forsworn. Isabella, naturally noble like Newman, accepts her Jewishness despite—indeed because of—her own suffering. As in his other Italian stories, Malamud uses Italy to illustrate the opaqueness of the culture to naive Americans, while depicting the problematic nature of freedom, entrapment in the past, and the need for his characters to "give credit" in whatever setting they find themselves.

Fantasies

Among Malamud's best stories are those that rely on fantasy for their effect. One critic has observed that when Malamud uses this method he portrays his characters through "a unique fusion of ground-gripping realism and high-flying fantasy, all seasoned by a tough, biting comic irony . . ." (Hershinow, 8). This fusion can be seen in "The Magic Barrel," "Angel Levine," "Take Pity," "The Jewbird," "Idiots First," "The Silver Crown," and "Talking Horse."

Both "The Magic Barrel" and "Angel Levine" are concerned with love and faith. In "The Magic Barrel" Salzman is almost as unreal as Levine the angel. Finkle imagines Salzman to be present even when not seen, a Cupid or Pan figure who may have planned his marriage to the fallen/innocent Stella. Neither Salzman nor Finkle understands love: Finkle learns about it through suffering; to Salzman it remains a piece of merchandise. For Malamud, "love comes not to the virtuous but to the vulnerable as a reward for revised expectations."[5] Salzman's Kaddish at the end is wonderfully ambiguous, as it may be for Stella's loss of innocence, or for what Salzman sees as Finkle's loss of innocence, or for Stella's immorality that makes her dead to her father, or for Salzman himself for having caused, in his eyes, Finkle's ruination. While it is not possible to view Salzman's Kaddish in a positive light given his limited perception, the ultimate irony is that he "pronounces death while the story celebrates life."[6]

"Angel Levine," like "The Magic Barrel," is both rooted in reality— the Job-like suffering, a poor apartment, a Harlem night club, Levine's "very large feet" that tie him to earth—and saturated with the fantastic—a Black-Jewish angel who appears from nowhere and flies away at the end. Both aspects are presented in simple, deadpan prose, with Yiddish-inflected diction and syntax and African-American dialect that creates humor in the juxtaposition of vernacular and colloquial speech patterns set against the extraordinariness of the situation. Manishevitz must make a leap of love and faith in accepting the desperate Levine as a genuine angel, as well as accepting God's unknowable ways.

"The Jewbird" and "Idiots First" are fables that stress the need for compassion in dealing with God's creatures, and both tales present the real and the fantastic as being virtually indistinguishable. "Idiots First" is reminiscent of "Take Pity" in its treatment of a supernatural figure as common and familiar, as a ticket collector or census taker. Mendel's success in using human values of love and sacrifice to defeat Ginsburg, the Angel of Death, shows that those values are very powerful, the implication being that they can even alter providential fate. There is a pessimistic note in the story, in that while Mendel can change the Angel of Death's decree, he fails to reach Fishbein's heart. But optimism lies in the rabbi's selfless charity, which shows that it is possible to "understand what it means human" (*IF,* 19).

Mendel's sacrifice of himself for Isaac is not paralleled in the bleakness of "The Jewbird," where Schwartz's death occurs out of hatred, fear, and genuine anti-Semitism on Cohen's part. As in "Angel Levine," a leap of faith—or acceptance of the perilousness of being different—must be made if Schwartz is to survive. Edie and Maurie make this leap; Cohen does not because of his desire to escape being Jewish and to assimilate completely. To accept the Jewbird—an outsider if there ever was one— would mean accepting his own heritage. In expelling the outcast, Cohen dissociates himself from being prey to "eagles, vultures, and hawks," and from having to search for an open window and charity. Taking on the phrases of the anti-Semite, Cohen loses any hope of redemption in Malamud's world and fails the test of compassion and humanity.

As in all the other tales, except "Talking Horse," that use fantasy as a device, Malamud uses Yiddish inflections to create both a sense of the ordinary and, particularly important in "The Jewbird," an understated humor. Schwartz's immigrant Yiddish accent is set against Cohen's Americanized vernacular, thus setting forth linguistically the distance between them culturally. As in Kafka's "The Metamorphosis," the story is so skillfully crafted that the reader readily suspends disbelief in his feeling of empathy for and acceptance of the moral tragedy depicted. Paradoxically, the Jewbird, particular in being both Jew and bird, encapsulates in his plight a much broader condition, the "sheer vulnerability of man to existence."[7] The fantasy is rooted in the commonplace, causing everything unreal to seem real.

In one of the best stories in *Rembrandt's Hat,* "The Silver Crown," the fantasy, which is dependent on the extent of the love of a son for his ailing father, verges on the miraculous. Having always neglected his father, Gans now feels guilt and desires his father's cure, not out of love but for self-expiation. The lack of love goes hand in hand with an inability to accept the validity of miracles. Gans sees Rabbi Lifschitz, whose Yiddish-inflected speech harks back to a world with different values than the secular American one, as a charlatan, not merely because he is presented as a subtly ambiguous character but because he represents those qualities of faith and unquestioned love that Gans lacks. Gan's lack of love for his father causes his father's death, the crown supposedly able to cure illness, not holding the key to the miraculous but to the love of one human being for another. There are overtones in the story of the mystery of love as seen in "The Magic Barrel" and "Idiots First," and of its lack in "The Jewbird." The issue of faith leading to miracles has also been explored in "Angel Levine."

Malamud uses a fantastic approach to explore the theme of the nature of freedom, and of what it means to be human, in "Talking Horse," a beast fable. The centaur that Abramowitz becomes has human aspirations tied to an animal's body; that is, everyone possesses a dual nature, no one is free, and Abramowitz has achieved his true humanity. In all of these fantasies, Malamud combines the real with the unreal and blurs the distinction between them. They are most effective.

Father-Son Stories

In addition to sharing a fantastic approach with many other tales, "The Silver Crown" also contains the important Malamud theme of failed father-son relationships. Both "My Son the Murderer" and "The Letter" also illustrate this theme in terms of a lack of communication, with the son in all three tales being most at fault, and all three ending on a bleak note. In "My Son the Murderer," Harry is similar to Gerald Dubin, the protagonist's son in *Dubin's Lives,* in his distance from his father and his detestation of the Vietnam War. His fear of the world has made him a murderer of human feelings, someone who can no longer trust or feel love for his father. Also without feeling is Newman in "The Letter." He fails to understand that although Teddy's letter is blank, it still signifies caring to Ralph, who receives the message of love from his son. Teddy constantly tries to "mail" the letter to his father, and it is this effort that shows that there is "plenty of news" on the blank sheets. Newman has never sent any caring messages to his father; he tries only to have a Sunday free from visiting him.

Socio-political Stories

When Malamud wrote "The German Refugee" and "Man in the Drawer" he was not a political activist. He believed that a writer makes his greatest contribution to political and social issues through his writing. In both tales, Malamud tries to show the human spirit in adversity, one suffering character making demands on a second, who, responding to them, experiences moral growth. In "The German Refugee" it is Martin Goldberg, Oskar Gassner's American-Jewish English teacher, who grows in human understanding through showing confidence in a victim of Nazism, even though he realizes through Oskar's suicide that he can never fully grasp what it means to be displaced. In "The Man in the Drawer," Howard Harvitz learns about human responsibility from the outcast Soviet writer, Levitansky. Like Gassner (a name with chilling overtones), Levitansky is prevented from expressing his "interior liberty" by an oppressive political system, and the story asks the question raised by Saul Bellow in *The Victim:* how far is one human being responsible for another? Levitansky says in broken English: "We are members of mankind. If I am drowning you must assist to save me" (*RH,* 72). Through giving aid to the writer, Harvitz earns his name change from Harris back to the original Jewish one and rejects the easy life his father desired for one of moral commitment, subsuming his own needs to those of another. Set against Levitansky's four stories that stress the lack of compassion in Soviet society, Harvitz's response to the writer's isolation and suffering gives ground for some hope. Both tales show Malamud's ability, seen most clearly in *The Fixer,* to use historical and political circumstances as essential elements in an elucidation of human character. Levitansky's courage, and Goldberg's and Harvitz's growth in human understanding, show the human possibilities that exist even amid tragedy.

A Basic Theme in "The Mourners" and "Rembrandt's Hat"

Undergirding the majority of Malamud's stories, whatever their other themes may be, is a concern with the difficulties of communicating deep-seated needs and inadequacies. This can be illustrated in two tales, an early one, "The Mourners" (first published in 1955), and a later one "Rembrandt's Hat" (first published in 1973). To Gruber in "The Mourners," Kessler's Kaddish is for Gruber's having become dead to human feelings. In fact, Kessler's prayer for the dead is really said for his own heartlessness in leaving his family years before. The superb irony in the tale lies in the humanizing effect that this misunderstanding has on Gruber. It makes him a mourner for his own moral shortcoming in having viewed the old man as merely a problem tenant and not a human being. Similarly in "Rembrandt's Hat," Arkin does not consider Rubin's plight as a middle-aged, mediocre sculptor whose wife has left him. Arkin's insensitivity lies in his not having weighed the effect of his remark concerning Rubin's hat's similarity to one Rembrandt wore, especially since Arkin was mistaken—and the hats were very different. When Arkin places himself in Rubin's shoes, he can bring himself to apologize. In both tales it is the need for sensitive understanding and compassion, difficult though they often are, that lies at the base of Malamud's vision of human relationships. An awareness of human needs is at the root of true communication.

Late Stories

The stories Malamud wrote in the 1980s, toward the end of his life, are not as effective as his earlier ones. Only "A Lost Grave" has a hint of the depiction of life's difficulties presented through an ironic humor. Malamud said in 1983: "I may have done as much as I can with the sort of short story I have been writing so long—the somewhat mythological, biblically oriented tales I have been writing. These become more and more difficult to do and I feel I must make a change."[8]

The change he moved toward was what he called "fictive biographies," a mixing of biography and fiction that carried "the meaning of the life as a short story" (Giroux, xv). He became interested in biography when writing *Dubin's Lives* and later produced "In Kew Gardens," about Virginia Woolf, and "Alma Redeemed," about Alma Mahler. The stories are interesting and the method shows some promise, but Malamud did not live long enough to develop it into an impressive form.

Looking back at the stories Malamud wrote over almost forty-five years, one perceives a continuity of concerns: "The themes are freedom, commitment, responsibility, and the bonds of love and hate that link man to man" (Helterman 1985, 129). His characters tend to suffer badly from life's tribulations; however, this suffering can in many instances spur a dormant conscience to acts of selflessness. Where this does not occur, Malamud makes us aware of the way in which circumstance can prevent the fruition of human possibilities. The stories, like his novels, show him to be a moralist first and foremost, in the tradition of Hawthorne and James, but one who frequently chooses the rhythms of Yiddish and the contours of the folktale. He is not totally reliant on these to create "wide ripples from very small disturbances" (Schechner 1987,

74), but this combination has produced some of his best tales. Further common themes are the imprisonment of a character in past limitations, problems of communication between a pair of characters, and the use of fathers and sons as opponents. Allegory and fantasy are forms he has found particularly fruitful. The best of his stories show Malamud to have been, in the words of his publisher, "a master of the form . . ." (Giroux, xv).

Chapter Eleven
A Postscript on *The People*

When Malamud died in 1986, he was working on Chapter 17 of a novel concerning a Jew who becomes chief of an Indian tribe called the People. It is modeled upon the experiences of the Nez Percé and Chief Joseph's attempts to save his tribe's land and his people from annihilation by the white man. Malamud became interested in the chief and his tribe during his 12-year residence in Oregon. Unfortunately, not only was the novel left uncompleted at his death, but no part of it had benefited from the author's revision, a particularly serious problem given the importance Malamud placed upon reworking his prose.

Had he lived, what might he have done with this version? Most likely he would have written several further drafts, since he stated that he produces "many more than I call three. Usually the last of the first puts it in place. The second focuses, develops, subtilizes. By the third most of the dross is gone. I work with language. I love the flowers of after-thought" (Stern, 63). Indeed, he said that he revised his works until the last minute. None of this was possible with *The People* and, as might be expected, the lack of revision shows, particularly in the unsubtle dialogue and the presentation of events in a manner that makes the reader aware of the heavy hand of the author manipulating the plot. Nonetheless, Malamud's craftsmanship is still frequently in evidence, though it would clearly be unfair to make any judgments concerning his artistry on the basis of this manuscript.

The protagonist, called Yozip until he becomes chief of the tribe, when he becomes Jozip, feels that he has a special destiny but does not know what it is. He speaks with a Yiddish accent that is recognized as Jewish by the whites but not by the Indians. When he is kidnapped by the People, the chief tells him: "Our ancestors said they were the children of Quodish. We live in his word. . . . We are descended from the first tribe."[1] The name Jozip is close to Joseph and alludes both to Chief Joseph and to the Joseph of the Bible, both of whom attempted to save a group of people who were undergoing great tribulations. Jozip chooses to change his allegiance and considers himself an Indian, a part of the

People. He sees the whites as liars, without morality in their unquestioned goal of expanding the land area of the United States regardless of
the rights of the Indians who were already there. The character called
Indian Head defines the policy of eminent domain as meaning that "the
strong man does what he wants. The weak man listens" (*TP*, 45).

The strongest parallel in *The People* with another of Malamud's works
is with *The Fixer*. The Jews in *The Fixer* and the tribe of the People are
both outcast groups in the eyes of the majority culture. Although the
former are attacked for political reasons and the latter for avaricious ones,
in both instances the majority believes in the inferiority and moral
depravity of the powerless group for reasons of self-interest. Both Bok
and Jozip are "chosen" as unwilling spokesmen for the oppressed, and
both change their names: Jozip to achieve his full moral identity, Bok in
an attempt to escape his. In the end the Jews survive as a people whereas
the People are destroyed, moaning as they are transported in freight
cars to a reservation whose land will not support their identity. Both
novels present obvious references to the Holocaust and to what end a lack
of conscience on the part of the powerful can lead.

This lack of conscience makes any communication between the U.S.
government and the People impossible, because the government will
give no "credit" to the Indians, desiring only to steal their land and
control their lives. His notes for the final, unwritten four chapters reveal
that Malamud planned to have Jozip go to night school to become a
lawyer and so try to help the Indians through other means. He planned to
end the book with Jozip doing a "'Hasidic' dance of the recovered self. A
rejoicing of life when the self seems annealed" (*TP*, 99). Malamud's son
Paul saw this ending as negating what might seem to be a despairing
novel. He wrote that his father "wished to conclude with a vision of hope:
Jozip was to plead the cause of the People before a nation rapidly
becoming more civilized. Malamud's theme is that words and thoughts
can conquer chaos, knowledge can conquer ignorance, ethics and law can
conquer barbarism. . . . Malamud believed the universe responds to
the human desire for justice" (*TP*, xiii).

Whatever one makes of this interpretation of Malamud's notes, the
planned ending is at best ambiguous and can be read as offering possible
redemption for Jozip, an individual who has learned altruism, but only
continuing catastrophe for the People, as the government has succeeded in
achieving its aims. The ending of *The People* follows the endings of *God's
Grace* and *The Tenants*, both of which present hope if one searches for it, but
perhaps the search is too difficult and the resulting hope too thin.

Chapter Twelve
Art Tending toward Morality

Malamud's work lies within the American literary tradition in that it is highly moralistic and frequently relies on allegory. This places him in the company of Hawthorne, Melville, Crane, Faulkner, and Hemingway, all of whom produced works that used a "'realistic' allegory wherein secondary meanings and their interrelationships are developed suggestively in an approach that is often ambiguous and frequently ironic" (Benson, 20–21). Hawthorne, of course, produced several more-traditional allegories—as in "Young Goodman Brown" and "The Celestial Railroad"—for example. Except for Malamud's beast fables ("The Jewbird," "Talking Horse," *God's Grace*), which constitute a special type of allegory, Malamud relied on more modern, highly suggestive forms that are less obvious in their symbolism. One critic observes that "in no way more than in his ability to view his characters as 'viewpoints' which look out on a greater allegorical reality does Malamud resemble his fellow American writers."[1] The use of characters that are realistic yet that also point to another set of correlated meanings is common in both Malamud's work and in American literature as a whole.

A divergence between Malamud's approach to character development and that taken by the majority of American authors can be seen in the maturity achieved by his protagonists. Tony Tanner notes that Malamud's novels depict "the painful process from immaturity to maturity—maturity of attitudes, not of years. This is unusual in American literature, which tends to see initiation into manhood as a trauma, a disillusioning shock, a suffocating curtailment of personal potential" (Tanner 1971, 323). For Malamud, moral growth leads to individual moral maturity, which in turns leads to a rejection of the success ethic of American society. Indeed, the attempt to achieve success through the acquisition of material wealth—one basis of the American Dream—makes the attainment of moral maturity through love and altruism impossible.

Although Malamud resisted the label of Jewish-American writer, his best work has what might be called a "Jewish" or Old Testament orientation. One commentator has described his greatness as being based upon a devotion to "Old Testament questions—Why should we be good, when there is no reward for goodness? How can we have faith, when there are no signs to confirm our faith? How can we love, if our love is met only with scorn or violence?" (Benson, 17). His concern for these questions found its most fruitful expression in his depiction of Jewish characters and their humanism. Helen Benedict sees Malamud's books as divided into two types: "The modern-life novels [*The Natural, A New Life, Dubin's Lives*], which are either not about Jews or are about men whose Jewishness is incidental to them, tend to be less believable, lively, or well-written than the others. . . . The Jewish books, on the other hand, *The Assistant, The Fixer, The Tenants, Pictures of Fidelman,* and his three volumes of short stories, are more poetic, moving, and humorous than the others. They are also the ones that have won Malamud his awards . . ." (Benedict, 32). *God's Grace* can be added to the latter list.

The effectiveness of the Jewish characters and their situations is directly related to Malamud's view of suffering. While many groups have experienced unjust suffering, Jews have had more than their fair share of it in their long history and, as noted many times in the course of this study, serve Malamud as representatives of the human condition, of the moral possibilities available to all humankind through accepting the inevitability of suffering and responding with increased love, mercy, compassion, and charity. Those who fail to learn the positive lesson of suffering, that all humanity is one, can never, in Malamud's view, achieve the secular redemption that is possible.

Malamud does not praise the existence of suffering or say that human beings should seek it out. Since it is there, it should be used as an aid to moral growth. His optimism can be seen in those characters for whom suffering leads to the realization of the best that is in them. Early in Malamud's career, one critic noted that his gentiles "though often portrayed as 'different,' are as harassed, as vulnerable as his Jews. Indeed, they seem to be mirror-image doubles, 'secret sharers,' as it were, in the centuries-old trail of blood, guilt, and recrimination."[2] All humanity shares the same adversities.

Malamud frequently uses the figure of the schlemiel, a victim with a comic aspect, to depict the human plight. This figure brings forth compassion rather than mockery and ridicule; pathos is the primary emotion elicited as the schlemiel's situation moves close to tragedy. Humor is an important device for Malamud, who, while he strips away all props from his suffering protagonists, frequently leaves them with resources based on irrational approaches to their problems. Their methods frequently work and show a perverse courage, as with Frank Alpine and Seymour Levin. Malamud's unlucky, naive fools often startle us as they overcome the ever-present victimizer who would thwart them or worse.

Pairs, victim and victimizer, are common in Malamud's writing, sometimes taking the form of a character's conscience, his doppelgänger, as with Fidelman and Susskind or Gruber and Kessler. Feelings that vary between attraction and repulsion are common, as the protagonist attempts to resist the finer demands of his inner self while also desiring their fulfillment.

The schlemiel figure, powerless and pitiable, grew out of the ironic situation of the Jews in history: their belief that they were chosen by God for a special purpose, contrasted with a daily situation in which they were treated as pariahs. This led to the creation of Jewish humor, which is highly ironic and "capable of sustaining hope while recognizing despair" in its incorporation of "both the tragic and the comic. As a moral perspective, Jewish humor combines the values of humanism with the gritty reality of an everyday life that seems existentially absurd. Malamud's use of Jewish humor provides the key to understanding both his attitude toward human existence and his technique as a writer" (Hershinow, 15). His attitude toward human existence and relationships is that they are uncertain, difficult, complex, and ultimately ambiguous; a comic, ironic approach is best suited to their elucidation.

The result of this approach is a stress on the distance between the actual and the ideal, between what is and what ought to be. A further stylistic application of this can be seen in Malamud's use of realism and fantasy, often in the same work; a tale may be rooted in the real world but move off into realms of imagination and fantasy that seem equally as real, as in *The Tenants* and "The Magic Barrel." One critic finds a "frustratingly unanalyzable blend of Yiddish fabulist, cynical realist, and fantacist of despair that is the voice of Malamud and only his: a miraculous verbal acrobat . . ." (Richman 1987, 211). Malamud himself described the "path" he takes in his writing as comprising "a feeling for people—real qualities in imaginary worlds" (Stern, 62).

Malamud's most commonly used point of view is the third-person omniscient, which permits him to present straightforward narrative information unknown by the character, and also to present the character's thoughts. This type of narrator has the freedom, unlike a first-person narrator, to ignore restrictions of distance and time and yet present the illusion of seeing the world through the eyes of the character. As with the first-person narrator, there is a sense of immediacy, but with a lack of restriction for the author.

Malamud's style has been seen by one critic as consisting of three parts: first, ". . . a 'straight' or standard belletristic style," which is not distinctive but similar to that used by other modern writers; second, a "dialect style which deliberately evokes the sound of Yiddish" and harkens to dialect styles used in American literature in the nineteenth century; and third, "a mixed or fused style which combines both the belletristic and dialect styles yet is wholly neither. Malamud can be named as the co-inventor of this style; he and Bellow began to use it at about the same time, in the early 1950's . . ." (Grebstein, 37–38). It is this fusion that gives Malamud's writing its stylistic distinctiveness. There is also a Hemingwayesque avoidance of embellishment that, unlike the style of both Saul Bellow and Philip Roth, eschews rhetorical language in favor of simplicity.

In terms of the novels, Malamud became increasingly pessimistic in the later works. There were signs of this orientation in the short stories and in *The Fixer;* however, *The Tenants, Dubin's Lives,* and *God's Grace*— despite Malamud's disclaimers about the final novel—all show that the achievement of altruism, of love, is increasingly difficult for his characters. This is especially noticeable when compared with earlier novels like *The Assistant* and *A New Life* and with short stories like "The First Seven Years" and "Angel Levine." While Malamud's characters have more possibilities for growth of conscience and morality than do those of, say, Philip Roth, his level of affirmation decreased.

This is not to say that Malamud altered his view of what is possible for humankind, perhaps only of what seems probable. He said in the early part of his career, after the publication of *The Magic Barrel:* "My premise is that we will live on. We will seek a better life. We may not become better, but at least we will seek betterment. My premise is for humanism—and against nihilism. And that is what I put in my writing."[3] This is more than the endurance that Faulkner spoke of in his Nobel Prize acceptance speech. It is closer to Saul Bellow's remarks, in his Nobel speech, concerning humankind having much more to it, having a spirit.

In 1975 Malamud expressed the view that art "tends toward morality. It values life." He added that "even the act of creating a form is a moral act . . . close to Frost's definition of a poem as 'a momentary stay against confusion.' Morality begins with an awareness of the sanctity of one's life, hence the lives of others. . . . Art, in essence, celebrates life and gives us our measure" (Stern, 51). This attitude helps to explain his belief that the so-called death of the novel is an illusion because the novel, when written by an artist who understands humanity's need for insights into the human condition, can provide an important vehicle for an elucidation of human experience.

Through most of his life, Malamud believed that the primary way in which an artist served humankind was through his art. He never lost this conviction; but his awareness of world problems—famine, population pressures, the slow spread of nuclear weapons, and political oppression—caused him to become involved in social activism while retaining his belief in the importance of art as a means of reminding people of the existence and importance of the human spirit. In 1979, when he reached 65, he said that he felt he ought to "use whatever renown I may have for some reason other than personal gratification." During that year, he became president of American P.E.N. and spent much effort in protesting "the repression of writers in the Soviet Union and South Africa, the rise of conglomerates in publishing and the curtailing of first Amendment rights."[4] In a writing career that spanned 45 years, he created a bittersweet image of humanity and what it is capable of despite, and often in response to, the oppressions of life. His voice is distinctive, his characters memorable, and his compassion great. His work will last.

Notes and References

Preface

   1. Sidney Richman, *Bernard Malamud* (New York: Twayne, 1966), 7.

Chapter 1

   1. Thomas Lask, "Malamud's Lives," *New York Times Book Review*, 21 January 1979, 43; hereafter cited in text.

   2. Curt Suplee, "God, Bernard Malamud, and the Rebirth of Man," *Washington Post*, 27 August 1982, F8; hereafter cited in text.

   3. Daniel Stern, "The Art of Fiction: Bernard Malamud," *Paris Review* 16 (Spring 1975): 56; hereafter cited in text.

   4. Leslie A. and Joyce W. Field, "An Interview with Bernard Malamud," in *Bernard Malamud: A Collection of Critical Essays*, ed. Leslie and Joyce Field (Englewood Cliffs, New Jersey: Prentice Hall, 1975), 12; hereafter cited in text as Field, 1975.

   5. Interview, *Jerusalem Post* (Weekly Overseas Edition), 1 April 1968, 13.

   6. Leslie A. and Joyce W. Field, "Introduction: Malamud, Mercy, and Menschlechkeit," in *Malamud: Critical Essays*, ed. Field and Field, 4.

   7. Leslie Field, "Bernard Malamud and the Marginal Jew," in *The Fiction of Bernard Malamud*, ed. Richard Astro and Jackson J. Benson (Corvallis: Oregon State University Press, 1977), 102.

   8. Charles Alva Hoyt, "The New Romanticism," in *Bernard Malamud and the Critics*, ed. Leslie A. and Joyce W. Field (New York: New York University Press, 1970), 171.

   9. Robert Ducharme, *Art and Idea in the Novels of Bernard Malamud: Toward the Fixer* (The Hague: Mouton, 1974), 93; hereafter cited in text.

   10. Samuel I. Bell, "Women, Children, and Idiots First: Transformation Psychology," in *Malamud and the Critics*, ed. Field and Field, 18.

   11. Philip Roth, "Writing American Fiction," in *Reading Myself and Others*, ed. Philip Roth (London: Jonathan Cape, 1975), 127; hereafter cited in text as Roth 1975.

   12. Jeffrey Helterman, "Bernard Malamud," in *Dictionary of Literary Biography: American Novelists Since World War II*, ed. Jeffrey Helterman and Richard Layman (Detroit: Gale Research Company, 1978), vol. 2, 291; hereafter cited in text as Helterman 1978.

   13. Israel Shenker, "For Malamud It's Story," *New York Times Book Review*, 3 October 1971, 22; hereafter cited in text.

14. Helen Benedict, "Bernard Malamud: Morals and Surprises," *Antioch Review* 41 (Winter 1983): 34.

15. Bernard Malamud, "'Living Is Guessing What Reality Is,'" *U.S. News and World Report,* 8 October 1979, 57.

16. Jackson Benson, "An Introduction: Bernard Malamud and the Haunting of America," in *Fiction of Bernard Malamud,* ed. Astro and Benson, 16–17; hereafter cited in text.

17. Ralph Tyler, "A Talk with the Novelist," *New York Times Book Review,* 18 February 1979, 33; hereafter cited in text.

18. Sam Bluefarb, "The Syncretism of Bernard Malamud," in *Malamud: Critical Essays,* ed. Field and Field, 78; hereafter cited in text.

19. Joel Salzberg, *Bernard Malamud: A Reference Guide* (Boston: G. K. Hall and Co. 1985), xviii.

Chapter 2

1. For further analyses of the mythological structure of *The Natural* see Earl R. Wasserman, *"The Natural:* Malamud's World Ceres," *Centennial Review* 9 (Fall 1965): 438–60; and Frederick W. Turner III, "Myth Inside and Out: Malamud's *The Natural,"* *Novel* 1 (Winter 1968): 133–39. Wasserman and Turner hereafter cited in text.

2. *The Natural* (London: Eyre and Spottiswoode, 1963), 33; hereafter cited in text as *TN.* All subsequent page references are to this edition.

3. Bernard Malamud, "Long Work, Short Life," *Michigan Quarterly Review* 26 (Fall 1987): 606.

4. Mark Goldman, "Comic Vision and the Theme of Identity," in *Malamud and the Critics,* ed. Field and Field, 163.

5. Jeffrey Helterman, *Understanding Bernard Malamud* (Columbia: University of South Carolina Press, 1985), 25; hereafter cited in text as Helterman 1985.

6. Jonathan Baumbach, "The Economy of Life: The Novels of Bernard Malamud," *Kenyon Review* 25 (Summer 1963): 443; hereafter cited in text as Baumbach 1963.

7. Sandy Cohen, *Bernard Malamud and the Trial by Love* (Amsterdam: Rodopi N.V., 1974), 27–28; hereafter cited in text.

8. Steven J. Rubin, "Malamud and the Theme of Love and Sex," *Studies in American Jewish Literature* 4 (Spring 1978): 20.

9. Edwin Eigner, "The Loathly Ladies," in *Malamud and the Critics*, ed. Field and Field, 95.

10. Sidney Richman, *Bernard Malamud* (New York: Twayne, 1966), 47; hereafter cited in text.

11. Robert Alter, "Jewishness as Metaphor," in *Malamud and the Critics*, ed. Field and Field, 31; hereafter cited in text as Alter 1970.

Chapter 3

1. *The Assistant* (London: Eyre and Spottiswood, 1965), 115; hereafter cited in text as *TA*. All subsequent page references are to this edition.

2. Allen Guttmann, *The Jewish Writer in America: Assimilation and the Crisis of Identity* (New York: Oxford University Press, 1971), 118.

3. Ruth Mandel, "Ironic Affirmation," in *Malamud and the Critics*, ed. Field and Field, 262; hereafter cited in text.

4. Iska Alter, *The Good Man's Dilemma: Social Criticism in the Fiction of Bernard Malamud* (New York: AMS Press, 1981), 13; hereafter cited in text as Alter 1981.

5. H. E. Francis, "Bernard Malamud's Everyman," *Midstream* 7 (Winter 1961): 94.

6. Ben Siegel, "Victims in Motion: The Sad and Bitter Clowns," in *Malamud and the Critics,* ed. Field and Field, 127.

7. Tony Tanner, "Bernard Malamud and the New Life," *Critical Quarterly* 10 (1968): 152.

8. William Freedman, "From Bernard Malamud with Discipline and Love," in *Malamud: Critical Essays,* ed. Field and Field, 164; hereafter cited in text.

9. Sheldon Grebstein, "Bernard Malamud and the Jewish Movement," in *Malamud: Critical Essays,* ed. Field and Field, 21; hereafter cited in text.

10. Peter Hays, "The Complex Pattern of Redemption," in *Malamud and the Critics,* ed. Field and Field, 233n; hereafter cited in text.

11. Walter Kaufman, "I and You: A Prologue," in *I and Thou,* Martin Buber (Edinburgh: T. and T. Clark, 1970).

12. Martin Buber, *I and Thou,* 54; hereafter cited in text.

13. Roth, "Imagining Jews," in *Reading Myself and Others,* 231-32.

14. Tony Tanner, *City of Words: American Fiction 1950–1970* (London: Jonathan Cape, 1971), 327; hereafter cited in text as Tanner 1971.

15. Ihab Hassan, "The Qualified Encounter," in *Malamud and the Critics,* ed. Field and Field, 205; hereafter cited in text.

16. Jonathan Baumbach, *The Landscape of Nightmare* (New York: New York University Press, 1965), 118; hereafter cited in text as Baumbach 1965.

Chapter 4

1. Marcus Klein, "The Sadness of Goodness," in *Malamud and the Critics,* ed. Field and Field, 249; hereafter cited in text.

2. *A New Life* (London: Eyre and Spottiswoode, 1962), 41; hereafter cited in text as *NL*. All subsequent page references are to this edition.

3. Leslie Fiedler, "The Many Names of S. Levin: An Essay in Genre Criticism," in *Fiction of Bernard Malamud,* ed. Astro and Benson, 154.

4. Ibid., 153. Fiedler remarks that Levin imagines "a West replete with

books and short on guns, a West different from the East only in lower density of population and greater beauty of scenery. He had no vision of the West as an alternative way of life, an altered mode of consciousness. . . ."

5. "Interview with Bernard Malamud," *New York Times Book Review,* 13 October 1963, 5.

6. "A Talk with Bernard Malamud," *New York Times Book Review,* 8 October, 1961, 28.

7. Astro and Benson, "Introduction," in *Fiction of Bernard Malamud,* 5.

8. Richard Astro, "In the Heart of the Valley: Bernard Malamud's *A New Life,*" in *Malamud: Critical Essays,* ed. Field and Field, 152; hereafter cited in text.

9. Theodore Solotaroff, "The Old Life and the New," in *Malamud and the Critics,* ed. Field and Field, 248; hereafter cited in text.

10. Giles Gunn, "Bernard Malamud and the High Cost of Living," in *Adversity and Grace: Studies in Recent American Literature*, ed. Nathan B. Scott (Chicago: University of Chicago Press, 1968), 65.

Chapter 5

1. See Chasia Turtel, "The Beiliss Trial," *Anti-Semitism* (Jerusalem: Keter Books, 1974), 197–98; and Maurice Samuel, *Blood Accusation: The Strange History of the Beiliss Case* (Philadelphia: The Jewish Publication Society of America, 1966).

2. Granville Hicks, "One Man to Stand for Six Million," *Saturday Review,* 10 September 1966, 37–38.

3. Haskel Frankel, "Bernard Malamud," *Saturday Review,* 10 September 1966, 39; hereafter cited in text.

4. *The Fixer* (London: Eyre and Spottiswoode, 1967), 352; hereafter cited in text as *TF.* All subsequent page references are to this edition.

5. John F. Desmond, "Malamud's Fixer—Jew, Christian, or Modern?," *Renascence* 27 (Winter 1975), 105; hereafter cited in text.

6. W. J. Handy, "The Malamud Hero: A Quest for Existence," in *Fiction of Bernard Malamud,* ed. Astro and Benson, 65.

7. Edwin Eigner, "The Loathly Ladies," in *Malamud and the Critics,* ed. Field and Field, 105.

8. Avindra Sant, "Surrealism and the Struggle for Identity in *The Fixer,*" *Studies in American Jewish Literature* 7 (Fall 1988): 185; hereafter cited in text.

9. James Mellard, "Malamud's Novels: Four Versions of Pastoral," *Critique* 9 (1967): 10.

10. Harold Fisch, "Biblical Archetypes in *The Fixer,*" *Studies in American Jewish Literature* 7 (Fall 1988): 164.

11. Elie Wiesel, *Messengers of God: Biblical Portraits and Legends* (New York: Pocket Books, 1977), 240.

12. Roth, "Imagining Jews," in *Reading Myself, and Others,* 235–36.

13. Saul Maloff, "Schlemiel Triumphant," *Newsweek,* 12 September 1966, 110.

14. Ben Siegel, "Through a Glass Darkly: Bernard Malamud's Painful Views of the Self," in *Fiction of Bernard Malamud,* ed. Astro and Benson, 123.

15. Maurice Friedberg, "History and Imagination—Two Views of the Beilis Case," in *Malamud and the Critics,* 279.

16. Jackson Benson, "An Introduction: Bernard Malamud and the Haunting of America," in *Fiction of Bernard Malamud,* ed. Astro and Benson, 22; hereafter cited in text.

Chapter 6

1. See Forrest L. Ingram, *Representative Short-Story Cycles of the Twentieth Century* (The Hague: Mouton, 1971), 15; and Warren French, *John Steinbeck: Revised Edition* (Boston: Twayne, 1975), 55, for a discussion of this genre.

2. Leslie Field, "Portrait of the Artist as Schlemiel," in *Malamud: Critical Essays,* ed. Field and Field, 124.

3. *Pictures of Fidelman: An Exhibition* (New York: Farrar, Straus and Giroux, 1969), 6; hereafter cited in text as *PF.* All subsequent page references are to this edition.

4. Ihab Hassan, "Bernard Malamud: 1976. Fictions Within Our Fictions," in *Fiction of Bernard Malamud,* ed. Astro and Benson, 51; hereafter cited in text as Hassan 1977.

5. Mark Goldman, "Comic Vision and the Theme of Identity," in *Malamud and the Critics,* ed. Field and Field, 161.

6. Field, "Portrait of the Artist as Schlemiel," in *Malamud: Critical Essays,* ed. Field and Field, 128.

7. Steven J. Rubin, "Malamud and the Theme of Love and Sex," *Studies in American Jewish Literature* 4 (Spring 1978): 21–22.

8. Robert Scholes, "Portrait of the Artist as Escape-Goat," *Saturday Review,* 10 May 1969, 34.

9. Roth, "Writing American Fiction," in *Reading Myself and Others,* 237.

10. Renee Winegarten, "Malamud's Head," in *Malamud: Critical Essays,* 100.

Chapter 7

1. *The Tenants* (London: Eyre Methuen, 1971), 55; hereafter cited in text as *TT.* All subsequent page references are to this edition.

2. David R. Mesher, "Names and Stereotypes in Malamud's *The Tenants,*" *Studies in American Jewish Literature* 4 (Spring 1978): 62; hereafter cited in text.

3. Cynthia Ozick, "Literary Blacks and Jews," in *Malamud: Critical Essays,* ed. Field and Field, 90; hereafter cited in text.

4. Leslie Fiedler, "Negro and Jew: Encounter in America," in *No! in*

Thunder: Essays on Myth and Literature (London: Eyre and Spottiswoode, 1963), 241.

5. Herbert Mann, "The Malamudian World: Method and Meaning," *Studies in American Jewish Literature* 4 (Spring 1978): 7.

6. Israel Shenker, "For Malamud It's Story," *New York Times Book Review*, 3 October 1971, 22.

7. Saul Bellow, *The Dean's December* (Harmondsworth: Penguin Books, 1982), 205.

Chapter 8

1. Ralph Tyler, "A Talk with the Novelist," *New York Times Book Review*, 18 February 1979, 31; hereafter cited in text.

2. *Dubin's Lives* (London: Chatto and Windus, 1979), 11; hereafter cited in text as *DL*. All subsequent page references are to this edition.

3. Sheldon J. Hershinow, *Bernard Malamud* (New York: Frederick Ungar Publishing Co. 1980), 104; hereafter cited in text.

4. Robert Towers, review of *Dubin's Lives, New York Times Book Review*, 18 February 1979, 1; hereafter cited in text.

5. Leon Edel, review of *Dubin's Lives,* in *Critical Essays on Bernard Malamud,* ed. Joel Salzberg (Boston: G. K. Hall and Co., 1987), 62; hereafter cited in text.

6. Daniel Fuchs, "Malamud's *Dubin's Lives:* A Jewish Writer and the Sexual Ethic," *Studies in American Jewish Literature* 7 (Fall 1988): 208; hereafter cited in text.

7. Rafael Cancel-Ortiz, "The Passion of William Dubin: D. H. Lawrence's Themes in Bernard Malamud's *Dubin's Lives, D. H. Lawrence Review* 16 (Spring 1983): 88.

8. James Mellard, "The 'Perverse Economy' of Malamud's Art: A Lacanian Reading of *Dubin's Lives,*" in *Critical Essays on Bernard Malamud,* ed. Joel Salzberg (Boston: G. K. Hall and Co., 1987), 189–90.

9. Mark Schechner, "The Return of the Repressed," in *Bernard Malamud,* ed. Harold Bloom (New York: Chelsea House Publishers, 1986), 182; hereafter cited in text.

Chapter 9

1. Helen Benedict, "Bernard Malamud: Morals and Surprises," *Antioch Review* 41 (Winter 1983): 31–32; hereafter cited in text.

2. *God's Grace* (London: Chatto and Windus, 1982), 4; hereafter cited in text as *GG*. All subsequent page references are to this edition.

3. Sidney Richman, "Malamud's Quarrel with God," in *Critical Essays on Bernard Malamud,* ed. Salzberg, 216–17; hereafter cited in text as Richman 1987.

4. Claude Rawson, review of *God's Grace, New York Review of Books* 21 (November-December 1982): 9; hereafter cited in text.

5. Elie Wiesel, *Messengers of God: Biblical Portraits and Legends* (New York: Pocket Books, 1977), 90; hereafter cited in text.

6. Clive Sinclair, review of *God's Grace, Times Literary Supplement,* 29 October 1982, 1188; hereafter cited in text.

7. Robert Alter, "A Theological Fantasy," in *Bernard Malamud,* ed. Harold Bloom (New York: Chelsea House Publishers, 1986), 189.

8. John Updike, review of *God's Grace, New York,* 8 November 1982, 167.

9. Robert Ottaway, review of *God's Grace, Listener,* 4 November 1982, 23.

10. Salzberg, *Malamud: A Reference Guide,* xx.

Chapter 10

1. Mark Shechner, review of *The Stories of Bernard Malamud,* in *Critical Essays on Bernard Malamud,* ed. Salzberg, 68–69; hereafter cited in text as Shechner 1987.

2. See *The Magic Barrel* (New York: Farrar, Straus and Cudahy, 1958); *Idiots First* (New York: Farrar, Straus, 1963), hereafter cited in text as *IF,* all subsequent page references are to this edition; *The Stories of Bernard Malamud* (New York: Farrar, Straus and Giroux, 1983); *Rembrandt's Hat* (New York: Farrar, Straus and Giroux, 1973), hereafter cited in text as *RH,* all subsequent page references are to this edition; and *The People and Uncollected Stories* (New York: Farrar, Straus and Giroux, 1989).

3. Sidney Richman, *Bernard Malamud* (New York: Twayne, 1966), 143; hereafter cited in text.

4. Guido Fink, " 'Ecco la chiave!': Malamud's Italy as the Land of Copies," in *Critical Essays on Bernard Malamud,* ed. Salzberg, 162.

5. Laura Krugman Ray, "Dickens and 'The Magic Barrel,' " *Studies in American Jewish Literature* 4 (Spring 1978): 39.

6. Irving Saposnik, "Insistent Assistance" *Studies in American Jewish Literature* 4 (Spring 1978): 15.

7. Ihab Hassan, review of *Idiots First, New York Times Book Review,* 13 October 1963, 5.

8. Robert Giroux, "Introduction," *The People and Uncollected Stories,* xii; hereafter cited in text.

Chapter 11

1. *The People and Uncollected Stories* (New York: Farrar, Straus and Giroux, 1989), 14; hereafter cited in text as *TP.* All subsequent page references are to this edition.

Chapter 12

1. Sam Bluefarb, "The Scope of Caricature," in *Malamud and the Critics,* ed. Field and Field, 150.

2. Ibid., 138.

3. Joseph Wershba, "Not in Horror but Sadness," *New York Post,* 14 September 1958, M2.

4. Michiko Kakutani, "Malamud Still Seeks Balance and Solitude," *New York Times,* 15 July 1980, C7.

Selected Bibliography

PRIMARY SOURCES

Novels

The Assistant. New York: Farrar, Straus & Cudahy, 1957.
Dubin's Lives. New York: Farrar, Straus & Giroux, 1979.
The Fixer. New York: Farrar, Straus & Giroux, 1966.
God's Grace. New York: Farrar, Straus & Giroux, 1982.
The Natural. New York: Harcourt, Brace, 1952.
A New Life. New York: Farrar, Straus & Cudahy, 1961.
The People and Uncollected Stories. New York: Farrar, Straus & Giroux, 1989.
Pictures of Fidelman: An Exhibition. New York: Farrar, Straus & Giroux, 1969.
The Tenants. New York: Farrar, Straus & Giroux, 1971.

Collections of Stories

Idiots First. New York: Farrar, Straus, 1963.
The Magic Barrel. New York: Farrar, Straus & Cudahy, 1958.
The People and Uncollected Stories. New York: Farrar, Straus & Giroux, 1989.
Rembrandt's Hat. New York: Farrar, Straus & Giroux, 1973.
The Stories of Bernard Malamud. New York: Farrar, Straus & Giroux, 1983.

SECONDARY SOURCES

Bibliographies

Salzberg, Joel. *Bernard Malamud: A Reference Guide.* Boston: G. K. Hall & Co. 1985. An extremely thorough and useful annotated bibliography to primary and secondary sources.

Books, Parts of Books, and Articles

Alter, Iska. *The Good Man's Dilemma: Social Criticism in the Fiction of Bernard Malamud.* New York: AMS Press, 1981. Useful study of Malamud's work in relation to social issues.
Astro, Richard, and Benson, Jackson J., eds. *The Fiction of Bernard Malamud.*

Corvallis: Oregon State University Press, 1977. Wide-ranging collection of essays, including one by Benson on a Malamud conference held in Corvallis, where Malamud taught for 12 years.

Bloom Harold, ed. *Bernard Malamud*. New York: Chelsea House Publishers, 1986. A recent essay collection containing some of the best older pieces as well as good newer ones.

Cohen, Sandy. *Bernard Malamud and the Trial by Love*. Amsterdam: Rodopi N.V., 1974. Convincingly discusses the important theme of love in Malamud's work.

Ducharme, Robert. *Art and Idea in the Novels of Bernard Malamud: Toward the Fixer*. The Hague: Mouton, 1974. Impressive study of a range of important themes.

Fiedler, Leslie. *To the Gentiles*. New York: Stein and Day, 1972. Good, often iconoclastic essays on Jewish writing; provides a background to the field.

Field, Leslie A. and Joyce W., eds. *Bernard Malamud and the Critics*. New York: New York University Press, 1970. Essay collection with three useful overview sections as well as essays on earlier works.

Field, Leslie A. and Joyce W., eds. *Bernard Malamud: A Collection of Critical Essays*. Englewood Cliffs, New Jersey: Prentice Hall, 1975. Good essay collection, including an interview with Malamud, an essay by the major Jewish-American author Cynthia Ozick, and a useful bibliography.

Girgus, Sam. *The New Convenant: Jewish Writers and the American Idea*. Chapel Hill: University of North Carolina Press, 1984. Interprets Jewish writers, including Malamud, in terms of ideas that underpin the American experience.

Guttmann, Allen. *The Jewish Writer in America: Assimilation and the Crisis of Identity*. New York: Oxford University Press, 1971. Good overall view of Jewish-American writers.

Helterman, Jeffrey. "Bernard Malamud." In *Dictionary of Literary Biography: American Novelists Since World War II*, vol. 2, edited by Jeffrey Helterman and Richard Layman, 291–304. Detroit: Gale Research Company, 1978. General discussion of Malamud's work.

Helterman, Jeffrey. *Understanding Bernard Malamud*. Columbia: University of South Carolina Press, 1985. Useful introduction to Malamud's work.

Hershinow, Sheldon J. *Bernard Malamud*. New York: Frederick Ungar Publishing Company, 1980. A study that provides some incisive observations within a tight format.

Knopp, Josephine Z. *The Trial of Judaism in Contemporary Jewish Writing*. Urbana: University of Illinois Press, 1975. Discusses the ways in which Jewish writers investigate Judaism, with a good chapter on Malamud's concern with moral growth.

Lasher, Lawrence M. *Conversations with Bernard Malamud*. Jackson: University Press of Mississippi, 1991. Collection of all Malamud's interviews.

Malin, Irving. *Jews and Americans*. Carbondale: Southern Illinois University Press, 1965. Good discussion of the early Malamud in relation to important themes in Jewish-American writing.

Malin, Irving, ed. *Contemporary American-Jewish Literature: Critical Essays*. Bloomington: Indiana University Press, 1973. Useful essay collection that includes overviews, a good bibliography by Jackson Bryer, and a wide range of pieces on individual authors and topics, including Malamud.

Richman, Sidney. *Bernard Malamud*. New York: Twayne, 1966. Good general study of the first half of Malamud's career.

Roth, Philip. "Imagining Jews." In *Reading Myself and Others*, edited by Philip Roth, 215–46. London: Jonathan Cape, 1975. Interesting essay criticizing Bellow and Malamud for not giving their Jewish characters more antisocial drive.

Salzberg, Joel. *Critical Essays on Bernard Malamud*. Boston: G. K. Hall and Co., 1987. Very good recent collection of reviews and essays.

Schulz, Max F. *Radical Sophistication: Studies in Contemporary Jewish-American Novelists*. Athens: Ohio University Press, 1969. Discussion of the complex ways in which Jewish-American writers have coped with the ambiguities of man in the twentieth century, including a chapter on Malamud.

Stern, Daniel. "The Art of Fiction: Bernard Malamud." *Paris Review* 16 (Spring 1975): 40–64. Very useful interview.

Studies in American Jewish Literature 4 (Spring 1978). Entitled "Bernard Malamud: Reinterpretations," this issue is devoted entirely to essays analyzing Malamud's work.

Studies in American Jewish Literature 7 (Fall 1988). Entitled "Bernard Malamud: In Memoriam," this issue is devoted entirely to Malamud's work, and contains what is probably his last interview and a useful bibliographic essay.

Index

The Author

Edward Abramson is a native of New York City and received his bachelor of arts degree from the City University of New York. He received a master's degree from the University of Iowa, then taught as an instructor in the English Department of East Carolina University, in Greenville, North Carolina. He researched his doctorate in England and was awarded a Ph.D. in English literature from the University of Manchester. Since 1971 he has been a member of the American Studies Department at the University of Hull, where he is a lecturer in American literature. In the 1986–87 academic year, he was Professor of English at the College of William and Mary, in Williamsburg, Virginia.

In addition to articles and reviews on literary subjects, he has published *The Immigrant Experience in American Literature* (1982) and *Chaim Potok* (1986).